Darren,

Wishing you all the
Best this season.

Burn The Ships

Michael
10/16/14

The Billion-Dollar Deal

Michael D. Maupin

Michael D. Maupin

Published by

ISBN-13: 978-0-9890925-0-0
ISBN-10: 098909250X

This publication is designed to provide authoritative information in regards to the subject matter covered. It is sold with the understanding that the publisher is not engaged in rendering legal, accounting, or other professional services. If legal advice or other expert assistance is required, the services of a competent professional person should be sought.

—From a declaration of principles jointly adopted by a committee of the American Bar Association and a committee of publishers.

Cover designed by

cheney ⧉ design
professional graphic communications

DEDICATION

Dedicated in memory of my mother who always told me to go read a book.
Look Ma, I wrote one!

CONTENTS

ACKNOWLEDGMENTS

I would like to thank my wife who continues to inspire me every day.

I would also like to thank Tab Edwards who motivated me to write this book.

Thanks to my editors, Jeannette Scott and Amanda Barnett for all of their wonderful advice.

To Brittany, Daddy is just trying to keep up with your success!

Thanks to Dean "The Reading Machine." I'm glad you approve!

Thanks to my proofreaders, Erin Todorovac and Clifford "The Glove" DeBaptiste for catching everything.

Michael D. Maupin

INTRODUCTION

When setting out to write this book, I had three objectives in mind:

1. To review the Consultative Selling concepts that my partner, Tab Edwards, and I teach at the Water Training Institute
2. To tell the story of how my team and I sold a $1.2 billion services deal
3. To write an interesting book

I couldn't complete the second item without also addressing the first since the reader might not fully understand our Consultative Selling process and how it was used to close a deal. But too much of the first objective would limit my ability to achieve the third. Therefore, I decided to meld the objectives together by highlighting the story of the billion-dollar deal with descriptions of different Consultative Selling methods.

The best way to fully understand the story is to read the book in sequence, from start to finish. While this book is based on true events, some names and details have been changed to better illustrate the sales concepts it contains. It is my hope that this story will inspire you and that these concepts will make you a more effective Consultative Seller.

I hope you enjoy the book.

Best Regards,
Michael Maupin

Burn the Ships

Facing an opposing army five times the size of his own, General Tariq saw defeat in the eyes of his men. As they stood watching, he ordered their ships burned. As the flames roared behind his army, with a rousing speech, he motivated his troops to fight. "I look into your eyes and I see the fear of women, not warriors! Women are to be protected. Warriors are their protectors. Look behind you one last time; for now, there is no return. Where you now stand, this land beneath your feet, is where you will die. But not today! We will win this war for our King, for our family and for our honor!"

In A.D. 711, an army of 12,000 troops led by General Tariq defeated King Rodrigo's army of 60,000. Gebel Tarik, or "the Hill of Tarik," is named in his honor. Today, it is known as the Rock of Gibraltar.

The Billion-Dollar Deal

1
INTRODUCTION TO CONSULTATIVE SELLING

When I was about 10 years old, I found an opportunity to fulfill my first customer order. My classmate, Gary, was one of the brightest and most passionate future scientists in my class. One day, our class went on a field trip to the local high school's biology lab. We conducted experiments, watched the lab rats scurry around inside their cages, and looked at all types of really cool stuff under the microscope.

Gary became so excited that he couldn't control himself. I don't remember how or why but he became obsessed with shrimp eggs and he wanted to acquire enough to hatch and raise them at his home. He offered to pay me 5 dollars a dozen if I could get him some. Without thinking, I said "yes!" That was more than my weekly allowance.

That night, I asked my parents, brother and sister how I could acquire some shrimp eggs. I had very little success. I was laying in bed that night thinking about my customer, the shrimp eggs and the 5 dollars. I couldn't sleep, tossing and turning much of the night. At school the next day, Gary asked me for the shrimp eggs because he had the money and I had to tell him that I didn't have them and didn't know if I would be able to fill his order. He seemed more upset than I was. I remember the sad look on his face and I knew I never wanted to be the reason a customer was dissatisfied again. On the bus after school, I thought about the deal during a loss review with myself. Like any loss review, I assessed what went wrong and how I could have prevented this customer failure.

And then it happened! I remembered my brother's microscope set. It had all types of interesting things in little vials with labels marking their contents, including one with shrimp eggs! I opened the vial, removed 12 shrimp eggs, wrapped them in a piece of aluminum foil and put them in my lunch box so that I wouldn't forget to bring them.

The next day at school, I almost jumped Gary with the shrimp eggs and closed the sale!

Later I learned the pitfalls of not understanding the cost of goods sold (my brother was not happy that I took his merchandise) and implications of poor product performance (two-year-old dried up shrimp eggs don't hatch!), but for the moment, I basked in the success of my first consultative sale.

Yes, consultative. I met with the customer, fully determined his needs, developed a solution to meet those needs at a mutually agreed upon price, and delivered a solution that, at least initially, resulted in high customer satisfaction.

Many salespeople have a similar story describing the rush they felt the first time they closed a deal. It's almost as if the gene is either in you or it's not. Although there are thousands of very successful salespeople who don't feel this rush in the same way, they do get a high level of satisfaction out of succeeding and winning. I draw this distinction to separate salespeople into two categories to better understand motivation:

1)   People who love the sale
2)   People who love the rush of seeing a satisfied
      customer

As you read the next section, think about what motivates *you* in a sales opportunity. Is it selling the product or satisfying the customer?

CONSULTATIVE SALES PHILOSOPHY

When I started in corporate sales, I didn't realize how fortunate I was to be selected. In those years, IBM had one of the best sales training programs in the world. Before a new salesperson sold one floppy disk (yes, I'm dating myself), he or she went through a 12 to 18 month training program. This training was based on the basics of a Consultative Selling model.

The best way to introduce Consultative Selling is with an exercise we conduct at the beginning of our sales training classes at Water Training Institute. The exercise is called "Sell Me an Orange" because I give someone one minute to close me on buying an orange. (For much more on this topic pick up Tab Edward's book *Lessons of the Naval Orange*.) When we ask a student to come up in front of the class and perform this simple sales act, we are measuring several things. First, how does the person react to being on stage in front of their peers? Being judged by one's peers is difficult because they know the game and what it takes to be successful. It's difficult to trick or fool your peers because they will know instantly if you have what it takes.

Second, within that one minute, did the student fall for the trap of pushing the features and benefits of the orange before they know if it will satisfy any of my needs? Because that's the point of Consultative Selling—you must first fully understand the needs of your customers before you can sell them a solution that will satisfy these needs.

But Consultative Selling is much more than that. The success of the Consultative Seller (or CS) is determined by his or her Attitude and Intelligence (A&I). A person's A&I determines his or her sales style and effectiveness. An effective CS comes in all shapes and sizes but the goal is to reach their impact zone. I will discuss the impact zone later but how the CS gets there is a matter of personal style.

As a CS, understanding your A&I will help you recognize your sales style. Recognizing your style will help you discover areas that need improvement and will ultimately make you a better CS. Selling style is a mixture of the components of a person's **Attitude**: Empathy, Aggressiveness, Confidence/Humility, Instincts/Intuition, Leadership and Communication. When these factors are combined with intelligence, a CS's effectiveness can be assessed.

Notice that I didn't mention things like happiness or positive attitude. These components are overrated. I've seen many salespeople with positive attitudes who sit around and wait for something good to happen. I've also seen many happy salespeople who don't care a bit about their customer. However, as long as the other components are involved, a happier and more positive individual will make a more effective salesperson. This list is not designed to be all encompassing because there are other components — like passion and balance — that are crucial to the success of any professional. However, because the A&I components are most important, we will examine them closely.

Attitude. This is a very broad and complicated topic that needs to be explored in greater detail. The Catlin dictionary defines attitude as "a complex mental state involving beliefs and feelings and values and dispositions to act in certain ways." I believe a salesperson's attitude is the most important factor in determining success. Your attitude will allow you to overcome your weaknesses and amplify your strengths.

I'm reminded of a story I heard at a business conference a few years ago. The speaker was describing the importance of attitude and used two twin boys as an example. They grew up in a tough inner-city neighborhood with no mother and a dad who was a drug-dealer. He provided no support, so the boys basically had to raise themselves. One boy went on to follow in his father's footsteps and ended up in prison, while the other worked hard in school and tried to live a decent life. This second twin would literally have to brush the drugs off of the kitchen table to do his homework. Despite this, he went on to graduate from an Ivy League school and become a successful lawyer. Each young man was interviewed and asked the same question. "How did your life end up this way?"

The twin in prison responded, "I ended up in prison because of my father. He was a drug dealer and that's all I knew how to be. It's his fault that I ended up this way."

When the other twin was asked, he replied, "Throughout my entire life, all I saw was what I didn't want to become. All my father caused me and my brother was pain and shame. I was motivated to work hard because I didn't want to end up like him. I became a lawyer because of my father."

This story is very interesting to me because you couldn't design a better test case for an experiment. They were two identical young men who lived in the exact same environment and were exposed to virtually the same motivations. However, one failed in life and the other thrived. Their attitudes were what made them different.

There are a number of different factors that contribute to a salesperson's behavior and therefore his or her actions with a customer. Since how these factors are utilized will determine a salesperson's success so let's explore a few important ones. I must note that the goal here is not to develop a personality test. Most of us have taken those with varying degrees of success. I am not a psychologist but, throughout my career, I have observed specific behaviors or skills that enable certain salespeople to be more successful with customers. Later, you will see how these skills were put into play to close multi-million dollar sales and, ultimately, the Billion-Dollar deal.

Empathy. Far too many people have the image of a salesperson as the obnoxious used car salesman or the smooth-talking guy in the three-piece suit who lies through his teeth. Sometimes these stereotypes do have merit, especially when the needs of the business force companies to pressure salespeople into delivering too soon. This can cause overly aggressive and pushy behavior. But, to be an effective CS, you have to understand your customer. Once you understand your customer's business, you can then develop empathy for his or her business problems. And empathy can't be faked. When you truly care, your customer will know. Later, I will discuss some of the techniques that I have used to immerse myself in my customer's business. When you are able to delve in that deeply, you can't help but learn how to serve your customer.

While a hammer is not the solution to every problem, the successful CS will know where to find the nails in his client's business. I'll admit that there are many successful salespeople working in various industries who only care about themselves. Contrary to the widely accepted adage, customers don't always buy from people they like.

I'm reminded of the time I went to purchase a car with my family. When we arrived at the car lot, my wife had to deal with one of our little ones so she told me to go ahead into the dealership. As soon as I walked in, a sales rep approached me and started in on his very weak spiel. He told me he had something I would like and walked me over to a popular sports car. When my wife came in with the kids, she looked puzzled. I then told the salesperson we had come to buy a new SUV. Before going to the dealer, I had done my research. I knew the car and features I wanted and I went to this particular dealer because it advertised that it would "Not Be Undersold."

In the middle of his sales pitch, it was agreed upon through eye contact between my wife and I that we didn't like him one bit. We found the car we wanted and he gave us their best price. He tried to close me but I told him I wanted to think about it and we left. Since we knew the car we wanted, we were making a decision purely based on price. Now that I had the specific features of the car, I could go shopping and it turned out that another location of this dealership had the best price in town.

So I returned to the first salesman and I told him I would buy if he could beat the price offered at the other location. And he had the gall to ask me why I had shopped the deal! It was obvious that he did not care about me and was only concerned with making the sale. I chose not to walk out because I have a personal rule that I will not let emotion control any aspect of my purchasing decisions. Unless someone says something to me that is intentionally or personally offensive, I'll buy from whichever salesperson has the best solution.

The salesman went through the usual negotiation routine with his manager and eventually beat the price. In the end, I didn't buy from the second location with a salesperson I liked because price was my motivation. I do believe in the axiom that people buy from people they like, but there are exceptions. You can't assume that the customer is going to buy from you just because you are empathetic. However, that salesperson's lack of empathy caused me to never go back to that dealership again.

Aggressiveness. This is another area where many salespeople miss the mark. They're taught to aggressively push and call high in the organization. This is obviously important but getting there the wrong way will only produce short-term success. Sometimes aggressiveness creates so many enemies that people within your account will begin working against you. I have seen this happen frequently throughout my career. We've all had customers come up to us and say "I want to help you win this deal because I can't stand the rep from XYZ." If you haven't heard that before, you might be the rep from XYZ!

Make no mistake, the successful CS does push a great deal, but they have earned the right to push. This is the basis for enacting change. When you have helped the customer and added value to his business, you've earned the right to ask for something in return, like an introduction to the CIO. Some salespeople think that asking for the order is an aggressive act. Not even close. If you have qualified the customer ("If I can show you a way to fix this business problem, will you buy our solution?") then asking for their business is a logical progression. The customer knows your request is coming and will often close *you* by asking for the contracts. If they don't, having met the customer's requirements, you have earned the right to ask for the business.

During many of our training classes, I'm frequently baffled by how weak even the most experienced salespeople are at closing the sale. Customers are busy and need help when buying from you. I've always believed in what I was selling or I wouldn't offer it to my client. Therefore, I feel a fiduciary responsibility to ensure that my customer receives the benefits of my solution. If it's a cost savings solution I'm selling, they are losing money until the solution is implemented. Because the customer is busy, the CS's job is to find the best way to get him to act. This is different for every customer. Knowing how to move deals through the customer's organization is the CS's responsibility.

Another important part of aggressiveness is one's ability to quickly bounce back from failure. Unfortunately, as CSs, we're in the failure business, so it takes strong drive and determination to keep pushing through tough times. If only we were able to close 50 percent of the opportunities that were identified, we could retire in five years or less. We may also lose a big deal occasionally. When this happens, we have to learn from the loss and quickly and aggressively pursue the next opportunity. Any lingering self-pity will affect our ability to win the next deal. It is no coincidence that many salespeople come from a team sports background because many of the characteristics of the successful athlete also apply to the successful CS.

As a CS, you work to add value to your customers. If your aggressiveness is not helping your customer solve business problems more quickly, then you might be pushing too hard. You can monitor your aggressiveness by constantly asking, "Is this move beneficial to my customer?"

Confidence/Humility. Customers like a CS who is confident. A salesperson who appears self-assured will put a customer at ease. Confidence comes from experience. It's important to present yourself as if you know what you're talking about because you have done it before is very important. In other words, if you don't appear to believe in yourself, why should the customer?

However, when salespeople cross the line and appear overconfident, they turn customers off. The "I know more than you" salesperson actually loses credibility the more he or she talks. The customer will wonder how the salesperson could know his needs if he hasn't asked about them.

Maintaining a balance between confidence and humility is the goal. Some salespeople have naturally more aggressive styles and need to turn up their humility factor. Others are just the opposite. The successful CS is self-aware and makes adjustments as needed. We all know what the unaware salesperson looks like.

Instincts/Intuition. I was rarely the smartest person in the meeting, but I often felt like I was the most intuitive. Intuition is what separates the good CS from the great one. Intuition is difficult, but not impossible, to teach. With the right training, I believe everyone can eventually become a more intuitive salesperson. As I will demonstrate later in the book, sometimes in the middle of the meeting, the CS's role is simply to read the audience and direct resources accordingly. We call that "running the meeting."

If you notice a client's questions or concerns, you should smoothly interrupt the meeting and address them promptly. The ability to do so is a valuable skill. While you don't want to disrupt the flow of the meeting or upset the speaker. You also don't want to put the client on the spot by forcing him to respond in an environment where he is uncomfortable.

The meeting flow should be discussed in the pre-call plan. The high sign—or nonverbal signal—for falling behind schedule or missing questions should be prearranged. Why is this important? The CS should possess an intuitive skill set so they instinctively know what his or her client is thinking better than anyone else calling on the account. The politics of the account, the dos and don'ts and knowing when a speaker is hitting or missing the mark are your responsibility. If the meeting goes well you get the credit. If it goes poorly, it's your fault. It's not always fair, but it's a responsibility that goes with the job.

Intuition includes knowing how job stress is impacting your client. During high-pressure times, the client might not be as focused on the deal you're presenting as you'd like. Pushing too hard could upset the customer and cause you to lose the deal. The stronger your relationship, the more you will earn the right to push. Later, I will illustrate times when I had to ask a great deal of my customer in order to close a sale. But I could do this because these relationships had been developed over several years. I had to provide a significant amount of value to my clients' businesses and their careers to ask for such imposing favors.

No one is perfect. Some of the deals I offered didn't bring the value my client and I believed they would at the time. That being said, I have never closed a deal that I didn't believe would help my client— at least not without disclosing it to my client first. What do I mean by this? One time my manager placed a $5,000 bonus on a deal using one of our new business solutions. It was a PC based application that also cost about $5,000. This solution didn't hurt my client, but it wasn't something I felt they needed. I explained to the customer why the deal was important because I had earned the right to ask for the favor. There was another way I could have approached this, however. I could have gone to this valued customer and tried to push this "wonderful new solution" on the client as a great benefit to their business. While I've seen many salespeople successfully use this approach, I don't believe that it is a successful long-term CS strategy. Over time, customers will recognize that you don't always have their best interest in mind and you will lose credibility.

Many salespeople are often faced with an age-old sales dilemma: Do I push what I'm forced to sell or develop solutions that my customer needs? The vast majority of the time, there is a mutually beneficial confluence between the needs of the customer and your sales directive. However, what do you do when management tells you that your green widget sales are too low but your customer needs blue widgets? Despite what you may have read, I'm not sure there is a right answer to this question. Earlier in my career, I was naïve enough to believe that everything we offered was best option for the customer. I developed business cases for these solutions and often won the business. Later, I realized that sometimes I was just carrying around a bunch of green widgets that my customer didn't need. I might be able to sell a few but, in the process, I could damage credibility and risk losing a larger opportunity in the future.

As I became an experienced CS, I learned more about my customer's business to better determine where my solution might fit. After a period of time, I understood my customer's business well enough to instinctively know when I could bundle a few green widgets together with another deal. If that option fails you, I recommend getting your manager involved. Explain the plan you've developed to sell green widgets that you believe moving forward, in this case, could damage your customer relationship. A good sales manager will understand the risks and cover you.

Like people, every company has a personality and a culture. And it is generally leadership that dictates the culture of every company. If a company's leader is a fiery, take-no-prisoners micromanager, much of that personality will permeate the entire organization. Understanding this environment and how it impacts each of its employees is very important. Some will fully embrace this culture and thrive, while others will struggle. The CS's job is to learn how to sell to the entire organization, one client at a time.

There is no single style that works for all customers. For example, some customers like to establish a good rapport before starting a meeting and might be turned off by salespeople that rush to get the meeting underway. If you assume all customers are the same, you'll get into trouble and may even be thrown out of some sales calls. My rule is to stay on the conservative side of the customer. If he is very outgoing, then you can be outgoing too, just never more than the customer. Also, you must respect the customer's time *even when they don't want you to leave.* I once had a customer who loved to talk sports with me. We would routinely spend over a half hour discussing the previous night's game. By the time we finished discussing business, I was well over the time allowed and this would put him behind schedule for the rest of the day. It got to the point where he would sometimes say that he didn't have time to see me and I realized that I had to regain control of our meetings. Less was actually more with this customer. Conversely, if your client isn't concerned with rapport, then start the meeting sooner than she would expect. I've found that customers that initially dislike small talk will eventually evolve into talkers. One of my least talkative clients once began a meeting with a 20-minute dissertation on tall fescue because I told him I was reseeding my lawn. (After that I had one of the best-looking lawns in the neighborhood!)

Sometimes the culture of an account will dictate your approach as well. For example, once when I was on a call, I was surprised to have a colleague point out a change in my behavior. My printer specialist, Kurt, and I were walking to my account and I was complaining that I was in a bad mood due to a business issue.

We happened to be visiting one of my favorite clients who was always playful and loved to have a good time teasing me and calling me by various nicknames. (My favorite was "Pay-per-View" because he said he only saw me when he was spending money. Of course this was not true but I played along.) When Kurt and I walked in, I unconsciously perked up. I started smiling and teasing everyone we saw. Later, Kurt said; "Who are you, the freaking mayor?" My change in personality was so sudden and dramatic that he thought it was an act. I didn't notice the change at the time but, later, I did realize that the culture of my customer was influencing my behavior just as it impacted its own employees. My personality was always a little more outgoing than normal when I was in that account.

The instincts of a seasoned CS are far more developed than a less experienced salesperson. The obvious reason is experience. After 25 years of selling to Fortune 500 organizations, I have seen virtually every type of customer behavior in a wide variety of situations. There are too many to list but when you consider this equation, you'll get the picture:

Number of Customer Calls x Type of Deal x Applied Knowledge = Sales Experience

If I conservatively assume that I have averaged just two calls per week during my career, that adds up to over 2,500 calls selling a myriad of hardware, software and services deals. The CS learns from all of his or her customer interactions and begins to apply this knowledge on future customer calls. As experience grows, the CS is able to influence sales calls to increase the percentage of positive outcomes.

We notice behavioral patterns when we are focused on observing and understanding these situations. We say things like "The last time I saw a customer this concerned with price, nobody won." I remember making a call with Linda, a senior sales representative, while I was in training. My role that day was to watch and learn and I was amazed by her knowledge and how smoothly she navigated through the call. The customer seemed to agree to everything she said and I thought the call went great. When we left the meeting, I was about to give Linda a high-five when she said, "Shoot. That was too easy. He's not going to do anything this quarter." She went on to explain in detail how a buying customer would be more aggressive with their objections before purchasing a solution like ours. "He agreed to the try-and-buy because he just wants to learn how the solution works. He probably lied about having the budget for it."

As she predicted, when she delivered the trial agreement, he backed out citing "new budgetary constraints." That is when I discovered the pitfalls of offering a customer a trial. A trial costs a customer nothing and is an easy way for them to try your product before buying. While it is low risk for the customer, salespeople are often tricked into believing they will buy simply because the customer is showing interest in their product. In reality, customers often use the product for a while to see if it will work and *then* try to convince management to buy it. This usually doesn't work and the product is ultimately returned. The salesperson has wasted time, money and effort on a situation that should have been avoided. Therefore, before initiating any trial, you should always qualify the customer with a trial agreement. This agreement simply states that the customer has the budget to buy the product and, if the trial meets the agreed upon objectives, the customer is obligated to do so. Customers who are just kicking tires will quickly admit they don't have the time or resources to devote to the project once they've read the trial agreement.

In Linda's case, her instincts told her that the customer was not serious. My instincts didn't because I hadn't experienced enough situations to recognize the behavioral patterns. Experience is different than knowledge. From a book, you can learn all of the details involved in delivering a baby. But until you actually see a baby being born, you don't realize how little you know about the topic. Because I have made a point of observing and learning from others over the years, I am now able to interpret the smallest details in a customer's behavior and use them to influence a purchasing outcome.

As you will see in the story of the Billion-Dollar Deal, when a CS walks into a customer's office, they are observing everything: the customer's appearance, how he greets the CS and shakes hands, how he interacts with others, how others interact with him, how his office looks, even the organization of his desk. All of this information is placed into a mental file that will be retrieved later. Sometimes I'm so focused on observation that I don't even hear a person's name.

After a while, a CS will instinctively tailor his or her style to suit the customer. We are trying to communicate with our customers and the more we can speak their language and respond to their behavior, the more effective salespeople we will be.

At the same time, however, we must continue to be ourselves. We have all seen the politician who does something out of character to connect with an audience and only comes off like, well, a politician. That is the main reason we use a pre-call plan as a guide instead of memorizing lines. People like to be treated specially whether they are at a restaurant or listening to your presentation. If you don't believe me, pay attention to the commercials that run during your favorite program. You will constantly hear phrases like, "Personal touch," "For you," "We care about you," and so on. The more you know about your customer, the better you can instinctively provide the personal touch that shows you care.

Leadership. Sales managers are constantly looking for new talent. Whenever I had an opening on my team, I always viewed leadership as a very important quality when considering potential candidates. At IBM, sales reps were ultimately responsible for everything that involved their customer. Although no one reported to them, they had to manage all the technical, administrative, and service personnel who interacted with their customer. They were like the quarterback of a football team. They called the plays and expected their fellow players to trust and follow them. If the running back missed a block, the quarterback would be in his face, letting him know it.

Ultimately, I believed the sales rep was the real manager. The more skilled he or she was at ensuring the team was doing its job correctly, the fewer problems I had to fix. I looked for people with a calm and steady leadership style because the reps who had a fiery, in-your-face personality seemed to lose control of their team over time. I also avoided the candidates who acted like they knew it all and tried to claim all of the credit.

It's like my father always taught me: no one knows everything. Sometimes it's best to let someone more knowledgeable lead. For example, in college, I took a class on organizational behavior. One day, our professor organized us into teams of four for an assignment. Each team was given a blank map of the world and asked to label 20 randomly selected countries on the map. Later, we learned his hypothesis: since he knew no one would be able to correctly locate all the countries on the map (they weren't random after all—he'd purposely picked obscure countries), he suspected the leader of the group would try to convince the other three to use his or her choices.

But during the exercise, I used a different approach. I did take control, but I wanted to find out who knew the most about each continent. I went around the group asking a series of questions to determine who I thought was the best person to make the decisions regarding that continent. We then went with that person's guess. After the exercise, we discussed the professor's view on leadership styles and how to spot a true leader. I didn't contradict him during the class, but not long afterwards I anonymously wrote a short paper in which I disagreed with his hypothesis and explained that the true leader would emerge by leading the group to the best possible answer. I asserted that a natural leader does not seek pointless control, but wants to win and will do what it takes to achieve a positive outcome. I told him I thought a leader is more concerned with getting it right than being right and that a domineering, loud-mouthed know-it-all is not a leader.

After class, I slipped my paper under the professor's door and walked away. At the beginning of the next class he seemed agitated. He read the paper and asked who wrote it. He said that he knew it had come from our class based on when it was delivered and then he paused, waiting for the author to come forward. I didn't budge. He then said, "That's too bad. Someone missed an opportunity for extra credit. That was an insightful and well-written paper."

After class I went to his office to take credit. He smiled and said, "I thought it was you, very nice job. But you're not getting extra credit. A true leader wouldn't remain anonymous." Lesson learned. The insight that I gained from this experience provided the foundation for my leadership style.

Communication. I think everyone would agree that communication is one of the most important skills a salesperson can possess. The ability to use oral, written and nonverbal communication to create the appropriate message is absolutely necessary to sell products, mold a company's image and create brand awareness. Communication is so important that the best-selling brands are most often the best-marketed brands. It is not uncommon to see the best-rated brand fall outside the top 10 in sales.

This was true in the personal computer space. In the early 1990s, there was a widely accepted belief (at least within the company) that IBM's PC operating system, OS/2, was more stable and reliable than Microsoft Windows. However, Microsoft did a masterful job getting independent software vendors to write applications specifically for Windows. This improved the functionality and value of Windows so customers were more willing to accept its instabilities. If you are wondering what this has to do with sales communication, who do you think was commissioned to communicate Microsoft's strategy to their customers? During that time, I personally saw many good IBM salespeople leave for successful careers at Microsoft. Their product strategy combined with a quality sales force made Microsoft a formidable competitor. Add this to IBM's unfortunate marketing missteps, and OS/2 didn't have a chance.

The effective sales communicator comes in many forms. Some are great stage presenters, while others are better one-on-one. It is natural for a salesperson to be more comfortable in one particular area, but the most effective CS will be good at all forms of communication. There are classes offered to improve these skills, but practice is the key. In my early days in corporate sales, I observed many great communicators. I watched them very closely and asked for advice. I was surprised to find how many of them routinely practiced in an office by themselves. I had believed they were naturally gifted orators who didn't need practice, only to find out the opposite was often true.

A frequently overlooked communication skill is the CS's ability to speak his or her customer's language. Whether the customer prefers e-mail or a phone conversation, the CS needs to be able to present information in a way that is reproducible throughout the organization. An e-mail that can be forwarded by the customer instead of summarized by him, will reach a wider audience more quickly. Moreover, using the customer's internal nomenclature for business and project terms will demonstrate your knowledge of their business. For example, there was a large package delivery company whose CEO hated it when the term "boxes" was used to refer to packages. He felt that boxes were empty while packages were full of their customer's valuables. Whenever he heard the word "box" used for package, he would get upset. You can imagine how he would receive this mistake in a sales presentation or proposal.

As a salesperson, the pinnacle of effective communication is when you hear your words repeated back to you by the customer. It's even better when the person repeating your words doesn't know they came from you. I was once in a client meeting with one of my product specialists when this happened several times. The project manager was using key phrases I had written on my deal sheet for a software opportunity, even though the meeting we were in had nothing to do with the software deal.

When we left the meeting, I told the product specialist that we had just won the software deal. I was right.

Intelligence. We won't spend a great deal of time on this topic because there have only been a few times in my career when I've seen a salesperson's intelligence as a stumbling block. I've seen people with very average intelligence thrive in sales and I've also seen brilliant people fail. In general, however, smarter people are more successful. If you possess a superior IQ, you should emphasize this strength in your selling style and in preparation for customer meetings. Before IBM hired a salesperson, the candidate was required to take an Information Processing Aptitude Test (IPAT). Not only was the IPAT designed to measure intelligence, it also tested the brain's interrupt processing ability. It was an extremely difficult test that required you to process different types of data simultaneously. Because, to be successful as a CS, you have to be able to design a technical solution while handling a phone call from an irate customer just as your manager asks you a question regarding your forecast. The average scores for most applicants were under 50 percent because IBM was looking for the next Einstein. If you aced the IPAT, you had a superior brain.

If you have a knowledge deficiency in a specific area, go fix it. Ongoing education is an important part of a CS's success, so when I say intelligence, I am referring to industry, product and customer knowledge. It takes work to stay current in these areas. The successful CS is constantly learning about his business and how to use new information to help solve business problems. The goal is to have an equal mix of technical, business and financial knowledge, though most people will gravitate more toward one of these areas. For example, [I'm stronger regarding business than I am the technical aspects]. As you will see later, while at IBM, I could bring in technical people but I needed to know the business better than anyone. Your approach needs to match what is right for you.

I don't teach style. I once managed a young sales rep who was replacing another rep I was promoting. The young rep was intimidated and couldn't fathom how she could replace the sales veteran, who held a Ph.D. I told her that she couldn't be him anymore than he could be her. She had to find the approach that suited her and, once she did, she'd have a very successful business career with a style nothing like the Ph.D's. I have seen managers make the mistake of teaching style. People fail when they try to be something they are not.

At Marketing and Business Integration (MBI), we do teach the mechanics of selling and what is important to accomplish in each phase of the process. For example, we recommend that the sale call begins with an introduction and small talk before jumping into a presentation. But we encourage students to play on their individual styles in order to be successful at this.

For example, some salespeople are comfortable telling a joke before presenting, while others completely fail at it. A poor joke-teller should not try to be Jerry Seinfeld if it doesn't come naturally. It's just like professional golf, where different athletes use various, yet effective, golf swings. But in the time right before and right after the golfer hits the golf ball, most professional golf swings look surprisingly similar. This area is called the impact zone. Being in perfect position during the impact zone is all that is important. In sales, how you get to your impact zone should depend on your personal preference because that is where you'll have the most fun. The impact zone is also where substance or intelligence meets style and produces a more effective CS. With too much substance, the CS can appear dull and robotic. And too much style can look fake and showy. The most effective CS has the prefect balance of personal style and subject matter expertise.

In summary, your A&I are critical to your success. Some of these skills are subtle, but it is my belief that they determine why some highly skilled professionals fail while their less skilled colleagues succeed. Since I believe some of these skills are the most valuable to the CS, I will employ many examples of how the A&I components were used while closing The Billion-Dollar Deal. You will also see how The Billion-Dollar Deal became the definitive "Burn the Ships" moment of my career.

2
THE OPPORTUNITY

The day started out like any other. I was a Business Unit Executive for IBM and I logged on to OMSYS, our sales opportunity management system, to review my region's year-to-date numbers. It was February 23rd, a little more than a month before the end of the quarter. Unfortunately, I was forecasting an $8 million shortfall on my first quarter number. [Add to that the pressure large corporations like IBM were feeling to give favorable showings to the Wall Street analysts each quarter and you get the stress I was under. This Wall Street squeeze was worse on us to make our quota each quarter than it had been to make our full year quota when I first started in the business.]

And this pressure from the top had resulted in the sales teams getting "help"—which was code for "you're being watched." I hated the new corporate micromanagement style that was permeating the culture of big business. It seemed counterproductive for two people to do the same job. I longed for the old days when, as a sales rep, I could look my new sales manager in the eye and say, "Stay the heck out of my account. I'll blow my numbers out and I'll call you if I need you." But I understood that the stakes were higher. A $500 million quota was a substantial piece of IBM and a poor showing in my territory could impact the entire company.

But this was the hand I'd dealt myself when I'd accepted a promotion two years prior. Now, I had to quickly come up with a credible gap plan to cover my $8 million shortfall or my boss, Scott, would be "sitting in my lap" by the end of the week. I had memorized all of the forecasts line by line from each of my team's territories and I was confident that each sales manager was in good shape to make their plans. My team always finished strong. They would sandbag until bonuses were set and then show their remaining cards. But I wasn't in it to just make a plan; the real money came from beating the quota.

I longed for another Y2K scare. The uncertainty that Y2K produced earned me a third Golden Circle Award for selling in the top two percent of the company. The Y2K scare had left every IBM customer in the world worried that planes would fall from the sky or bank accounts would vanish if their mainframes couldn't account for the 20XX date format. The 19XX format had worked just fine for years, but the brainiacs who designed software must have thought the world of computing would cease to exist in the new millennium. It ended up being an overhyped scare that did nothing but funnel billions of dollars into the Y2K consulting industry. It also helped me make 143%

of plan! That award came with a nice bonus and a two-week cruise down the Mediterranean coast with stops at many of the finest cities in Europe.

I knew, however, that this year was going to be very different—it was going to be a blocking and tackling year. I would have to watch every $20,000 piece of hardware, software and service through the stages of the sales cycle like a stockbroker watches the crawler. I would have to follow the Consultative Sales Cycle diligently and repetitively. *Identify, Qualify, Build the Business Case, Close. IQBC, IQBC, IQBC ...* That acronym raced through my mind over and over as I read each forecasted line item. Each letter represented criteria that had to be met before the opportunity could successfully move on to the next stage. If a salesperson had an opportunity in the Qualify stage, he could expect me to grill him to be certain of it. I never accepted anything falling out of the forecast after the Qualify stage. If it did, it meant the opportunity had not truly reached that stage and should not have been pushed forward. I understood when things slipped a month or two, but when a territory frequently experienced deals falling out, it was a reflection of poor territory management and I quickly made a change.

Block and tackle, keep territory expenses down, focus on the numbers, conduct frequent pipeline reviews, and allow absolutely no MIA time on the golf course, or sailing, or wherever my team went at 3:00 p.m. on a summer

Friday. They knew this would be a year that I would have to account for every moment of their time. They wouldn't have as much fun, but if we reached 105 percent of plan, I'd have enough holiday bonus money to pass around and appease the ranks. I convinced myself that this was for the team's own good. If I made my sales quota and grew the business, there would be no grim reaper coming to layoff any of my people!

Barb buzzed my phone, "Call on line two." Barb Stanley was my assistant. She had been at IBM for more than 25 years and had watched me develop from my first day in the Finance and Insurance Branch.

Now, 10 years later, I often recall how lost I felt on that first day. During a branch meeting of 150 employees, I was introduced as the new trainee. Louis Sutterfeld, the IBM branch manager, seemed like a king. I was amazed at the power he seemed to wield over all of his super-impressive employees. Barb was Louis' assistant and we seemed to hit it off from day one. She made sure I got in to see Louis whenever I wanted. Now, since IBM reorganized, as a Business Unit Executive, I ran that branch plus the equivalent of two others. But in the new IBM, the Business Unit Executive didn't have the same prestige as the former branch manager title.

I snatched up the receiver. "This is Mike Maupin," I chimed.

"I think I've got something," a familiar voice said. It was John Hardy, one of my best sales managers who only called when things were either very good or very bad. I would sometimes answer his calls by asking, "Which is it?"

Coming from someone else, this opening statement could mean anything. Coming from Hardy, it meant something big ... really big. He never needed help with his deals and only told me about them after he knew they were qualified.

Hardy explained that his small customer, DialTex, was considering a move to outsource all of its IT operations. As he spoke, I did some quick math in my head, tallying what might be included: data center, call center, help desk, application development, and more. This could be a $500 million, five-year deal! Maybe more!

My heart pounded as I grilled Hardy with my usual qualifying questions: *Who said it? What's the timeframe? Why? Cost cutting? Who else knows?*

Every answer confirmed this was for real. As my heartbeat quickened, I could feel my entire body coming to a heightened sense of awareness.

"Hardy, we have to get in front of this with an action plan *now*. The competition will be all over this and the internal vultures will disguise themselves as helping hands and circle our deal like prey."

It was 4:00 p.m. and Washington, D.C., was a two-and-a-half hour drive with traffic. "I'll be there at 5:30," I told Hardy. While I never needed much of an excuse to blow the carbon on my 911 Carrera, this certainly qualified as one.

Hardy laughed. "I'll make reservations at Sullivan's," he said.

I had an administrative assistant and a remote office in our D.C. building. I always kept a bag packed and my clubs in the car. There had been too many times over the years when I had to get to the airport, New York, or D.C. stat. Going home to pack would take an hour and that cost me a deal once. I vowed that would never happen again, and certainly not this time.

I remembered from Hardy's last account review that DialTex was struggling. The Wall Street Journal and the trade rags had run articles on the company's financial woes. Understanding DialTex's play—their motivation for potentially going forward with this deal—was my primary focus. After years in the business, my training and experience had made me very process-driven. And my process was that there is no Point B; it doesn't exist, until Point A has been achieved.

This opportunity was in its infancy. It had not been qualified and therefore was not yet a deal. The first step in the Qualification Stage is to determine the play. Is it a financial play, such as cost savings? Do they want to appear more stable? For example, many companies sell outsourcing as a way to show Wall Street that they are focused on their core competencies. They tell the analysts, "Let the IT professionals do what they do so that we can do what we do." If Wall Street likes this story, the stock goes up. If it doesn't seem plausible, the stock goes down.

DialTex needed a game changer. As a provider of cellular technologies, their products, service and support were a distant third, or worse, when compared to AT&T and Verizon. Their biggest competitive advantage—push-to-talk—was great for construction and road crew applications. But there weren't a lot of business executives lining up to have a walkie-talkie on their cell phone. I realized that IBM couldn't help DialTex with product innovation. But cost reduction and the ability to free up manpower in order to improve customer service and operational efficiency were areas where IBM could play. And, a multi-year partnership with IBM consultants who could help DialTex expand their internal operations might look good to the street.

So there it was, the play. I wrote it down:

1) Cost reduction

2) Improved customer service

3) Process reengineering

Initially, this was the customer motivation my team and I would sell internally when the skies darkened with so-called "help" and interrogation. In general, and especially with highly visible deals, the account team has to display an image of control. We would say, "Of course we anticipated this opportunity. We think they are doing it for the following reasons."

I developed this strategy after receiving advice early in my career from a senior sales rep named Mike Forgash. Mike had retired as a Captain in the Navy with 20 years of service before starting with IBM. He had already spent 25 years with IBM when I started with the company. The awards and medals he had received over his two careers could fill an office and he had met many world leaders and famous entertainers. And yet, he seemed unaffected by any of his accomplishments. His two favorite topics were his two sons and *you*, the person he was helping.

When he developed cancer and had to retire, Mike's farewell speech was one of the most indelible memories of my career. Mike had barely started when he broke down and had to go back to his seat. There wasn't a dry eye in the room. The branch manager thanked him and was preparing to continue the meeting when Mike stood up and said, "If at first you don't succeed ..." His speech chronicled a life so full of memories it seemed unbelievable—unless you knew him.

Mike became a mentor of mine early on. I had been at IBM three weeks and realized that I knew nothing. At branch meetings, I would hear colleagues present ideas and data I could barely follow.

"How are things going?" Mike asked me. I shared my concerns.

"It's your first job and it's normal to feel overwhelmed in the beginning. Besides," he said, "IBM is a world unto itself and complexity is its goal. The talent lies in the person who can wade through all of the career-enhancing displays and showmanship to find out what is true, valuable and important." He went on to explain that it is important to find one's niche and become an expert in that area. He loved sports analogies.

"Are you a pitcher, or a centerfielder?" he asked. "You can't be both. But whatever position you feel is right for you, be the best!"

I took this advice. I knew that I was not, nor ever would be, a techie. The technical brain trust at IBM was second to none. I recalled the results of one of the many personality assessments I had to take and realized that what I enjoyed the most was also where I was my best: the business, the deals and the customer. From that day forward, I resolved to be the best at knowing my customer and the inner workings of IBM. As a result, I would be the best at creating ways to get deals done. I could bring 1,000

Michael D. Maupin

colleagues to my account to discuss an IBM solution, but if
I brought in anyone who knew my customer or their
business better than me, it would be a problem.

I decided the best way to know the customer was to be
the customer. I attended new employee training for my
three major accounts. I also attended company picnics,
softball games and even a few internal meetings. I lived
and spoke like my customers and was ultimately accepted
as an insider. When negative industry news was
announced, I felt my customers' pain. When one client
reached a revenue milestone, I celebrated at the client's
party. When another client's CEO had a book signing, I
was in line with the "other" employees, my copy in hand.
My access to information was so freely available it was
almost unfair to the competition. My clients knew that I
cared about their business; you couldn't fake that level of
commitment. They also cared about my business and
wanted me to do well. Most of my clients knew *my*
business so well that they would actually ask about my
quota at the beginning of each year. As a result, I only
missed my objective once as a rep and was recognized with
the Golden Circle Award four times for being in the top
two percent of sales worldwide.

As I experienced all of these achievements throughout
my career, I would often reflect on the conversation with
Mike Forgash. I knew it was the seminal moment that had
lead to my success. When I won the coveted Mike Forgash

Award for Rep of the Year at the branch meeting, I also received a trophy that then had to be returned to the office showcase. The second time I won it, I never gave it back. It has remained on display in my office ever since and I have no plans to return it. Since that type of recognition is no longer promoted at IBM, I knew it wouldn't be a problem. During important deals, I would often pluck Mike's trophy and listen to the cup ring for good luck.

I was sometimes called a control freak. Before anyone called on my account, I prepared a list of do's and don'ts to which some took offense. I didn't care. After having to clean up so many mistakes made by people who had called on my account, deciding to upset a colleague instead of my customer was an easy choice to make. [Besides, colleagues who followed the rules of my accounts usually did very well.] I even went so far as to tell the new sales manger I reported to that I didn't want him calling on my customer. At IBM, the first line sales manager didn't wield enough power to be important to the customer. They usually only called on customers when there was a problem or simply to conduct a routine check-up. I believed there were no IBM sales managers on the planet that could solve problems in my account better than I could. To be fair, I offered the same deference to sales reps when I became a Sales Manager and Business Unit Executive. I usually only called on customers when asked by either the account team or the customer.

As Hardy and I evaluated the opportunity across the dinner table that day in D.C., I leaned in and said, "We're ready for them."

Consultative Sales Cycle (IQBC)

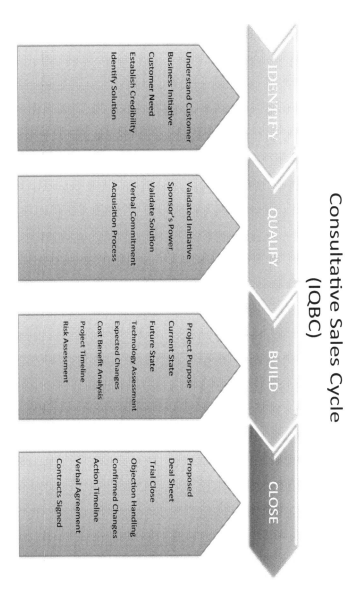

IDENTIFY
- Understand Customer
- Business Initiative
- Customer **Need**
- Establish Credibility
- Identify Solution

QUALIFY
- Validated Initiative
- Sponsor's Power
- Validate Solution
- Verbal Commitment
- Acquisition Process

BUILD
- Project Purpose
- Current State
- Future State
- Technology Assessment
- Expected Changes
- Cost Benefit Analysis
- Project Timeline
- Risk Assessment

CLOSE
- Proposed
- Deal Sheet
- Trial Close
- Objection Handling
- Confirmed Changes
- Action Timeline
- Verbal Agreement
- Contracts Signed

THE CONSULTATIVE SALES CYCLE

Before our story continues, it's important to understand the Consultative Sales Cycle. The Consultative Sales Cycle is designed to be very easy to follow. Each stage of the Consultative Sales Cycle must be completed before moving on to the next one.

IDENTIFY

Understand Your Customer: Before any opportunity can be identified, the CS needs to have an in-depth understanding of their customer's business. No one should understand your customer better than you. Spend time researching their products, industry and competition. Also watch and learn the politics of the company. Who are the power players? Who are the decision-makers, recommenders and influencers? Connect with inside sales representatives—client sponsors who support you and will assist your efforts by providing insight, influence and direction.

Business Initiative: Each year, companies establish their business initiatives. Many of these objectives are stated by the CEO in the annual report. Within each quarter, public companies provide insight as to how well they are doing against these objectives. All of this information can be easily researched on the Internet and in trade journals. Staying current is very important. Your customer's business frequently changes to adapt to external trends.

Customer Need: Once the customer's business has been fully researched, you can begin identifying solutions to meet the customer's needs.

Establish Credibility: You are now ready to demonstrate your knowledge by having discussions with the customer regarding their needs. This establishes credibility and prepares the customer to receive your ideas. Your identified solution is introduced to the customer and a buy-in is established. You begin working on the Initial Benefit Statement.

QUALIFY

Assessing whether or not you have a qualified opportunity is a critical step. Working on unqualified opportunities wastes a great deal of time because the disqualifier may not impact the opportunity until later in the Consultative Sales Cycle. For example, let's say you are working on a deal that your client likes and wants to buy. During the next three weeks, you bring in technical resources to develop the solution. When your client goes to get approval, you learn that your solution is not in the client's budget. Knowing this upfront would have saved a great deal of time and company resources.

Validated Initiative: The identified solution is discussed with the CS's technical resources. The CS has further discussions with the client and looks to gain buy-in from additional customer contacts in order to validate the customer's initiative.

Sponsor's Power: Determine the sponsor's power in the organization. Has he or she done a deal similar to this in the past? Is the client a recommender or decision-maker? It's important to understand your client's access to power if an additional approval is needed.

Validate Solution: Develop and present a conceptual view of the solution to the customer that includes an estimate of the proposed products and pricing of the solution. Ensure that both your technical resources and the customer agree with the concept.

Verbal Commitment: Use a qualifying question to gain a verbal commitment from the customer. In other words, request that, if you are able to develop a solution that meets the customer's needs and produces their desired benefit, they will buy the solution from you. Establish the conditions and timeframe of the sale with the customer.

Acquisition Process: Verify that the customer has funding to buy the solution in the agreed upon timeframe. Determine if the product will be leased or purchased and if any special conditions like price discounts or deferred payment will be required. **Validate the approval**

process and ensure that the client holds the authority he thinks he does.

BUILD

Building the Business Case is the most important stage of the Consultative Sales Cycle. Because Consultative Selling often involves moving larger and more complex solutions, the scrutiny and analysis of these deals requires greater customer participation. The approval process usually reaches a higher level in the organization so the business case must be created with the C-Level in mind. ("C" stands for "chief", as in chief financial officer or chief information officer.)

Project Purpose: The Project Purpose must be tied to the customer objective that was determined in the Identify stage. If there is no clear purpose, it is unlikely the project will succeed. Proceeding to build the business case won't be effective until the customer establishes a project purpose with you.

Current State: This is a benchmark used to establish and document current business problems and the current environment. When compared to the future state, it validates the benefits of the proposed solution.

Future State: After an analysis of the current environment, the recommended future state is developed and the benefits are compared to the current state.

Technology Assessment: This is an analysis of the proposed solution to determine if it is compatible with the customer's existing environment. Technology changes are recommended and tested to meet the customer's approval.

Expected Changes: The recommended solution is evaluated to see if there are any physical or environmental modifications necessary. If this is the case, the costs of these changes are incorporated into the cost-benefit analysis.

Cost-Benefit Analysis: The expected benefit of the proposed solution is analyzed to determine if the investment is a good financial decision. Common metrics like Return on Investment (ROI), Present Value and Payback Period are calculated.

Project Timeline: The implementation plan of the proposed solution is presented to the customer. The customer agrees to an installation timeframe.

Risk Assessment: Potential risks of implementing the proposed solution are listed. A contingency plan for each risk is developed.

CLOSE

Closing the sale should be fun. If you have done the previous steps correctly, the Close is a logical progression that the customer expects. Often the customer will beat you to the Close and ask for the contracts.

Proposed: The proposal is delivered to the customer. A **Deal Sheet** that summarizes the proposal is presented to the customer. The opportunity costs of not acting are clearly defined. The **Trial Close** is completed.

Objection Handling: The customer's questions and concerns are addressed.

Confirmed Changes: Business, political and economic changes that could impact the customer's decision are discussed. All assumptions are validated.

Action Timeline: A decision date is established and the customer's next steps are confirmed.

Verbal Agreement: The customer agrees to buy the proposed solution and requests the contracts.

Contracts Signed: The deal is closed.

3
THE HELP

"Cambull is coming when?!" Hardy shouted.

Bill Cambull was IBM's superstar CEO. Seven years prior, when the company was headed for corporate disaster, Bill was hired by the board to turn things around—and that he did. Using his no-nonsense approach, he cut the fat and dismantled the pompous culture. He endorsed the perspective that our 13 individual IBM companies were assets, not liabilities, by creating synergies among them and streamlined operations by using the strengths of one asset to offset the weaknesses of another.

For such a powerful CEO, he could be surprisingly down-to-earth. I vividly remember that the first time I met Bill was at a roundtable. The IBM roundtable was a staged event where the CEO visited a location and invited some of the company's future stars to sit down for a roundtable discussion. Originally, the roundtables were intended to bring the CEO closer to the business, the customer and any employee issues all at once. About twelve employees were supposed to roll up their sleeves and honestly and naturally share their ideas with the CEO.

But, over time, the roundtable had turned into a spectacle. On one visit to Philadelphia, the previous CEO—who traveled with an entourage that would rival the Queen's—was very particular about the appearance of his buildings. All along the route he and his entourage would travel throughout the building, the site manager had to have the walls painted and the floors waxed. Before the meeting, participants were coached not to present anything problematic or confrontational. Instead, they were either given questions to ask or told to pen their own career-enhancing comments for the CEO's pleasure. The roundtables had become a joke—the CEO gleaned no actual business insight from them and employees didn't get any problems solved.

Bill's style was so different that it took some by surprise. One roundtable I attended was featured in the *Wall Street Journal*. It was held in the IBM office in downtown Washington, D.C., where Bill showed up on the fifth floor by himself and went straight to the front desk. He told the receptionist that he was there for the roundtable. She explained that he was early and asked him to take a seat because Mr. Cambull wouldn't be arriving until 11:00 a.m. He looked at the receptionist and calmly said, "I am Bill Cambull."

The receptionist stumbled and stammered so desperately that Bill had to calm her down. "It's okay," he said. "You're fine. Just tell me where the conference room is and I'll be okay."

What the Journal didn't report was what went on inside the conference room. As the twelve of us sat around the table, my colleagues and I did our normal competitive assessment of each other: "He looks sharp", "She speaks like a player", "I wonder what his title is", "I'm better than him, him and her, but that guy seems very strong."

At the same time, the perceptive attendees also noticed that something felt different. Our previous CEO would have 8 to 10 "dogs" (our term for the administrative assistants being groomed for their next executive position by carrying briefcases, fetching coffee and taking notes for their master) trailing around after him. Bill only had two. I realized that I had better read Bill quickly if I was going to grasp his style. I desperately hoped I wasn't going to be the first one called upon.

After the usual introduction proceedings, Bill jumped right in with a question for the unluckiest person in the room. He asked Jack Huffier, an Ivy League-golden-boy-kiss-up, how he thought things were going in his region. Jack went through the standard rehearsed IBM soliloquy which included so much innocuous rhetorical praise of the company that previous CEO's might have applauded. Based on the old standards, it was quite worthy, but it became painfully obvious that Bill wanted to set a different tone for these roundtables.

Bill paused, stared directly at Jack and said, "I'm not sure what that even means." Bill then looked at me and asked, "Mike, you said in your introduction that you were from the Mid-Atlantic region?"

"Yes, Philadelphia."

"You guys are piloting the pay-for-profit tool. How's that going?"

I realized Bill wanted my honest opinion and that he wasn't attending these meetings to get long-winded answers. I also sensed that I would have to support my response with examples.

I began, "On the surface, it is working well. Reps are now being exposed to the impact of the total cost of delivering their solution, including shipping, configuration mistakes and payment terms. Reps are now reducing these costs because errors are reducing their commissions. The one problem is that some mid-range machines are producing more absolute profit than mainframes. If higher commissions are leading us to sell more of our smaller machines, our topline revenue growth could be affected. Conversely, our PC business could suffer because both the profit and revenue are very small."

I thought, *home run!* My answer was not entirely off the cuff, however, because I had been told that Bill might ask about our pay-for-profit tool. But since I didn't have to go first, I altered my response when I assessed that Bill didn't want cake, he wanted steak—rare.

Before Bill could respond, some techno digit head thought the time was right to use my PC response to ask Bill's opinion of our PC operating system vs. Windows. Bill paused and stared at him. His pauses were uncomfortable and his stares were penetrating. He reminded me of the Terminator when he scans his victim to assess the best means of attack.

And then he responded, "I don't want to talk about *that!*" He turned and pointed to me, "You, continue!" That moment would go down as one of the most intimidating experiences of my career.

When I finished, Bill thanked me and continued on to his next target. I called my wife on the drive back to Philly and said, "I don't know if IBM can be fixed but if anyone can do it, I believe Bill's the one."

But Bill Cambull coming to DialTex was a problem. In the midst of working on winning this deal, my team and I had to take a week off and prepare a briefing document. That was the minimum amount of time these exercises usually took, but I refused to put my team through that burden. The last time we had to prepare for a Cambull visit was for a deal at National Bank. We had 30 day's notice and used most of it. During the limo ride from the airport, Bill was presented with a 25-page briefing document replete with charts, graphs, and revenue projections related to the National Bank deal. Key points of emphasis and problem areas were highlighted. Bill flipped through the document, spending no more than a few seconds on each page. As the team members watched, we looked at each other with one collective thought: *"I can't believe we spent all that time on this just to watch him nonchalantly flip through it!"* However, after signing a copy of his book sheepishly presented to him by National's CIO, Bill masterfully ran the customer meeting, quoting every germane fact and figure as if he had prepared for hours. That's when I realized that Bill was a speed-reader with a photographic memory. I later told my team that Michael Jordan was built for basketball and Bill Cambull was built for business.

Bill's visit to DialTex would be different. National Bank was a $200 million deal. Although large, it wasn't one of the company's first billion dollar deals. Everyone of substance at IBM hated to lose, but Bill hated it most of all. Several times I had witnessed what I considered to be the biggest flaw in Bill's management style: public executions.

Normally, when the CEO hosts an employee meeting in a region, there are 3,000 to 5,000 in attendance. It's a real "rah-rah" festival, a pep rally of sorts. These meetings usually coincided with the winning of a big deal, and the account team was brought up on stage and recognized with cash awards. However, on many occasions, Bill also chose to highlight the ill-fated account teams that had experienced untimely, major losses. Bill was kind enough not to have them stand but everyone already knew who they were because that kind of news spread quickly in the company. If anyone had missed the news flash, Bill would oblige, providing the name of the account and the size of the deal. He would invariably end with the painful question, "How could this happen with all of the resources at IBM?"

It was very awkward. Most people would search through the audience to find the account team and witness their reaction, then try not to stare. Those few uncomfortable moments were tough for everyone. I knew all of the teams and, most of the time, there was little that could have been done to avoid the loss. As long as there are choices available to customers, there will be losses. We sat in our chairs and thought, "I hope I *never* find myself in their position."

And that was the point.

On one occasion, it had been my duty to help organize one of these meetings, which meant I was seated near the front. At the end of the meeting, Bill exited stage left and I overheard as one foolish member of the executed party felt compelled to approach Bill backstage and tell him that he didn't know the whole story and that his accusations were unfounded. One of Bill's dogs tried to gently escort him away before Bill could hear, but it was too late. Bill turned around and walked slowly toward his prey until they were nose to nose. While piercing a hole through his head with a laser-like stare, he coolly and softly said, "I don't have a problem with anything I said. Are we clear?"

As Bill left for his limo, one of his administrative assistants pulled the poor soul aside and conveyed the obvious, "You probably shouldn't have done that."

He never recovered and was gone three months later.

While I was on the phone with Hardy, Barb buzzed to inform me that Dick Tomlinson's office was on line two. I put Hardy on hold and learned that Dick, not Bill, would be calling on DialTex. This was not a real surprise because, six months earlier, Bill had announced his retirement and named Dick as his replacement. [For a deal this large, stability and continuity at the CEO level would be important to the DialTex relationship.] Also, Dick knew DialTex's COO, Tony Gaudenza (a former IBM-er who left on fair terms with the company when he realized that Dick was the heir apparent.)

"Great!" Hardy despaired, "This freaking deal is doomed."

It was no secret to Hardy that I didn't like Dick. Although extremely effective, his micromanagement style represented everything I thought was wrong with IBM and Corporate America in general. I was a huge Bill Cambull fan and wished he could remain CEO for another six years. I recalled Bill and Dick's announcement tour where they laid out the transition plan for our customers. I attended the Philadelphia leg with one of my large customers. In typical Bill style, he came on stage with nothing but a microphone and a wooden stool. He spent 45 minutes captivating the audience with a recap of his vision for IBM and where he thought the future of Information Technology was headed. The audience gave him a standing ovation. Then he introduced Dick and two jumbo screens on either side of the stage aired an IBM commercial. Dick took the audience through a PowerPoint presentation full of the customary graphs and key bullet points. At the end, my customer looked at me, smiled and said, "I'm going to miss Bill."

The last thing we needed was Dick

micromanaging this deal. We needed a plan.

"Okay, look Hardy, we need to get out in front of this and fix the calendars," I said. Fixing calendars was a common ploy we used to delay meetings. We would get available dates from Dick's office first. Then we would check DialTex's availability and somehow ensure that none of the dates matched. Back in my sales representative days, when I'd attempt this, my customers would ask if this was someone I didn't want them to see because they understood the game. This ploy could backfire if Dick's team ever tried to schedule with DialTex directly. But we had to risk it because we needed time to determine if there was any bad blood between Dick and Tony Gaudenza. When Gaudenza left IBM was he upset that Dick got the job? Did Dick throw it in his face?

"Can you get Jenny to take her time with this?" I asked.

Jenny was Tony's assistant and Hardy knew her, but not very well. He agreed to try to buy us a week for due diligence but, during that time, things became red hot. Dick's request to call so early in the deal's sales cycle caused the process to accelerate. All the "help" started calling me and Hardy to get involved. Because the deal consisted of hardware, software and services, there were multiple sales specialists in each of these areas that needed account briefings and direction. I decided to have a conference call with at least 25 IBM-ers.

Hardy gave a general account update and a high level overview about the opportunity.

"It is a full outsourcing opportunity," he said. "DialTex plans to have the winner of the bid install and run their data center, call center, and application development. Also a few other items could be in play, like process reengineering and a long-term product development partnership. This is a billion-dollar opportunity."

There was no use delaying the inevitable. The size of this deal had to come out and the repercussions of its exposure would soon be felt. We were now IBM famous.

THE CONSULTATIVE SALES BIG 5

The Big 5 model is my approach to running a business. My territory planning process systematically measures each component of the Big 5 to determine where improvements are required. An improvement plan is developed for each area. Notice the location of the CS circle. Like most consultative salespersons, I've been accused of thinking that the world revolves around me, but in this process it must.

CS Big 5

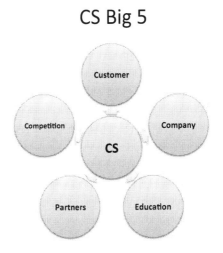

Customer

Every aspect of the planning process is designed to bring value to your client. No one should know your customer better than you. Develop your approach to learn the intricacies of each one of your clients. Become a partner instead of a vendor.

Company

Learn the most effective ways to navigate and manage your company resources in order to best serve your customers. This includes your manager, product specialists, administrators, call center support, etc. Everyone who touches your customer impacts you. You are responsible for their actions. Manage their effectiveness and select the best people.

Education

Obviously, product and industry education is a must, but also assess your strengths and weaknesses. For example, if you view public speaking or financial selling as weaknesses, take classes to improve these areas.

Partners

The CS provides complex solutions to their customers. Very few companies are able to do this without business partners. These partners have to be managed as an extension of your team. Since many business partners will sell your competitor's products as well, you need to select those that will serve your best interests while in your account.

Competition

Learn your competitor's strengths and weaknesses. Know who is calling on your accounts and when. Develop strategies to block their penetration. Never disparage the competition in front of your customer. In fact, I usually never mention the competition. If a competitor is weak in a particular area, I highlight our strengths in that area. I have seen too many salespeople embarrassed by presenting competitive data that turned out to be outdated.

4
THE PLAYERS

After several calls to former teammates, managers and other contacts, Hardy and I began to develop a much clearer picture of the relationship between Dick and Tony. While there was no bad blood between them, they weren't exactly sharing cookie recipes either. Dick would have to tread lightly and respectfully. Any underlying tone of "I know what's best for DialTex" would be disastrous. Leaders of multi-billion dollar international firms have egos as large as movie stars. Dick would have to show deference to the customer; however, if Tony tried to dangle this deal over Dick in a power play, it would be equally detrimental.

The format for the meeting between them was one-on-one. There would be no administrative assistants on either side taking notes or offering advice. All we could do was wind Dick up and let him go. If you have never witnessed this type of sales call, it is a treat. They typically start with the usual pleasantries and eventually graduate to an all-out praise fest where they applaud how each other handled their company's public business activities recently discussed on Financial Broadcast Company, (FBC). It's almost like they're in an exclusive club that deals with pressure and power no one else understands. When one former colleague described it, he said it was as if Larry Bird watched Magic Johnson play basketball on TV the previous week and then they met to discuss the game. No one else could understand them because no one else *was* them.

The briefing went well. Dick had been on top of most of the DialTex news prior to our meeting. We discussed the normal account history, past revenue streams and future projections. Hardy was granted the task of putting Dick's ego in check so that he didn't screw up. This was done through his administrative assistant, of course. We weren't fools. To be blunt, Dick could sometimes be volatile. Stories of how Dick's temper could erupt during meetings with his team floated around the company. One such rumor surfaced just after IBM missed a quarterly forecast. Apparently, Dick and his team were sitting around the conference room table when something set him off, causing him to pick up a candy dish and hurl it across the room. It crashed against the wall, launching shrapnel everywhere. One person took a shard of glass in the face. His wound was dressed and the meeting continued. Later a rule surfaced that nothing that could be used as a projectile could be left on the conference room table.

Hardy coordinated the logistics of getting Dick and his team to the DialTex headquarters for the meeting. We were very nervous that day because, as of that moment, everything was out of our control. We had to rely on Dick to do what he was told—something which executives rarely do. Hardy waited outside with Dick's administrative assistants and shot the breeze while Dick and Tony met for about an hour. When the door finally opened, Dick left too quickly. There wasn't the normal lingering and chitchat customary to a meeting gone well. Later, in the debrief call, we found out that the meeting didn't go badly, though this was certainly not going to be a relationship sale for IBM. There were no plans for any follow-up meetings and the word came down to me from my VP of sales: Do not lose this deal! Typically, a sales executive calls on your account, lays an egg and relieves himself of all responsibility—and we were just fine with that. While the less involvement we had from IBM's executive team the better, we didn't really think that they would ever leave us alone on a deal this big.

The next day, I called a meeting with the insiders of Hardy's account team. I gave my best Burn the Ships and Knute Rockne "Let's win one for the Gipper" speech, [explaining that we were put in a horrible situation.] "Dick messed up and now they're looking for someone to blame because they think we might lose this deal," I said. "There is no turning back now. I know we can win it. I know we *will* win it because we are strong and our careers depend on it!"

When you can sell it, the "us against the world" message is very effective for motivating just about any kind of team. In this case, it was an easy sale because IBM had turned into a difficult place to work. Dick's highly tactical, micromanagement style had changed the culture within the company to such a degree that it would no longer have been recognizable by our founder. One of the three beliefs the founder instituted for IBM employees was respect for the individual, but, unfortunately, the poor economy didn't allow companies to focus on anything but the bottom line. We had dissolved our full employment practice a few years prior and layoffs were as rampant at IBM as they were in Corporate America as a whole. Those fortunate enough to have a job had to stop complaining, work harder and be thankful to have a job.

The problem for IBM-ers was that Dick's style was producing results. IBM did need to trim the fat to become more efficient and profitable, and the Wall Street analysts loved him and thought he could do no wrong. But employee moral was at an all-time low and we knew that losing this deal would be devastating to all who were directly involved.

The stage was set. We knew the game, the team was in place, the customer had clearly laid out its objectives for this initiative and our competition was obvious. There were other competitors, but this deal would come down to IBM and GDS. The rule was clear: win by any means necessary. We had about six months before DialTex would make a decision.

Over the next three weeks, we worked quickly to develop an integrated solution. No single company could deliver on all of DialTex's requirements so we had to find partners. Due to the visibility of this deal, we were being inundated with phone calls, e-mails and stop-ins from dozens of companies claiming to have the best solution for a particular requirement. Fortunately, it was up to IBM Global Services to make most of the partnering decisions. They knew this space well because it was all they did. Even so, we had to stay involved in the selection process because we had to sell their solution to DialTex. Any potential partner that might have had a troubled past with the customer had to be deleted. That was *our* job.

One of the greatest coincidences on this deal occurred during the selection of a partner to run the call center. Establishing a call center was a huge component of the overall solution and represented about a third of the total revenue. There were three companies under our consideration and the Vice President of Sales for one of them was my next-door neighbor.

One of the most important facets of selling that I stress in my training classes is the human aspect. We cannot deny its importance. The human aspect shows up in deals in several ways. Sometimes it's revealed when a sales representative is uncomfortable unleashing his or her personality in front of the customer. Other times, an overinflated ego results in a pushy sales representative whom customers don't like. Frequently, personal life dictates a person's attitude, which influences behavior. Being self-aware and honest about how you are being received by the customer is a valuable skill that is often difficult to acquire.

In this case, the human aspect was my next-door neighbor and golf buddy, Dennis, who wanted me to help his company. His company was a fraction of the size of IBM and winning this deal would set records for them. As a result, he was also under a great deal of pressure and subconsciously tried to place his pressure on me. *Great*, I thought, *someone else who needs managing*. I was at capacity and I had to quickly handle Dennis.

Over the course of my career, I had experienced other situations in which there were overlaps between business and personal relationships, so I had learned how to manage them. For example, early in my career, I had a friend named Lav, who was assigned as one of my account administrators responsible for orders and billing. Although he was a highly skilled administrator, Lav was often late with orders and his work contained careless errors. There were times when he made me look bad in front of the customer because of his mistakes. In the office, it was not uncommon to hear me laying into him so fervently that no one believed we could ever be friends again. And, if one of these incidents occurred on a Friday, our colleagues were especially baffled by the sight of the two of us having a great time together that evening at happy hour.

What they didn't know was that I had struck a deal with him. In order to remain friends, I made him agree that what we did between 9:00 and 5:00 would have no bearing on our relationship after work. I actually got this idea from a Saturday morning cartoon I watched as a kid, which starred Ralph E. Wolf and Sam Sheepdog. Each episode began with Ralph greeting Sam as they punched the time clock in the morning. After they hung up their coats and set down their lunch pails, their workday began. Ralph's job was to attack the sheep while Sam's job was to protect them. Their attacks and counter attacks were rivaled only by the battles fought between Coyote and Roadrunner. Each episode concluded with one about to murder the other as the end-of-the-day whistle sounded. Immediately they would stop, clock out, shake hands and say "Goodnight." There would be the normal office talk about evening plans as the screen faded to black. The irony of seeing them trying to kill each other in one instant and suddenly shaking hands in the next was hilarious.

The moral of that cartoon was that, in business, we all have a job to do. Sometimes it means stepping on toes or dressing down a co-worker when he is out of line, if it's for the good of the company. It isn't personal. It's the job. Most reasonable people will understand when your objectives and actions run counter to theirs. The big problems occur when you are too weak to communicate your position. So when Dennis accidentally spilled his bucket of problems on me, I immediately had to act. I knew that there would soon be appeals for information, access to IBM Global Services executives and other special requests thrown my way. So I got in front of it and explained to Dennis that the importance of this deal was causing a great deal of stress on both of us. If we were going to remain sane friends and neighbors, we would need to separate our business and personal relationships. Of course I would like the call center business to go his way, but I would not jeopardize my business for the sake of his.

I wish I could tell you that was all it took to control Dennis. Over the next few months, I would have to remind him several times. He would push the limit until I sounded the whistle and then he'd quickly back down. It was almost like a game we played. We respected each other's position, but make no mistake, in sales, access to decision makers is imperative. Even with the rules I placed on Dennis, his relationship with me gave him a significant competitive advantage over the other two companies vying for IBM's business. At a minimum, he received information quicker than his competition and I'm sure I unknowingly slipped information to him that his competition never received.

One of our lead services managers was John Buchannan. John and I had worked together for several years so there was a great deal of mutual trust between us. He was competent and I didn't have to worry about him trying to compromise our customer relationship. We reviewed several potential partners, discussing their pros and cons, and I always felt like we were on the same page when deciding with whom we should work. But what he would do during this deal would take me completely by surprise.

SWIMMING IN THE DEEP END

The process of becoming effective in sales is a lot like learning to swim. When my daughter, Brittany, was 6, she took swimming lessons at summer camp. She was a quick study and grasped the concepts of swimming very easily. She focused on the task without fear. At birth, babies have a natural and instinctive ability to swim that comes from their nine-month lease in the womb. Toddlers are comfortable and playful in the water. We only begin to fear swimming after we learn the dangers of the swimming pool and the necessary safety rules: no running, no swimming right after eating, always swim with a buddy, and stay in the shallow end. Learned fear then begins to control our actions. But as a child takes lessons, she slowly unlearns this fear and begins to play freely—in the shallow end of the pool. More practice and successful skills tests bring encouraging words from adults, "You're almost ready to swim in the deep end!"

In most controlled learning programs, students are trained in the shallow waters of the classroom where the risk of failure is low. In this environment, they feel safe to act naturally. The problem with most training programs, however, is that they miss a very important step. Without addressing the fear of failure, these controls continue to place limits on students by restricting their ideas, personality and creativity.

However, sometimes it's best to dive into the deep end and risk sinking or swimming when learning a new skill. I come from a family of swimmers, and my father taught the old-school method: jump in deep water and paddle for your life. I was four years old and had complete trust in my

Michael D. Maupin

dad. So when he said he would be ready to rescue me if I needed help, I leaped without hesitation. I fought the water for a while, and then dog paddled like mad toward the side of the pool.

"Dad! Help!" I gasped when I grew too tired to reach the side. His firm hand grabbed my arm and guided me to the ladder nearby.

Water slid off me as I climbed out of the pool and wiped my eyes. "I can swim!" I shouted, jumping in the air. I'd always had a healthy respect for the water, but now I had the confidence to conquer it. I developed a natural confidence in my ability. I played in the shallow end but learned courage and skill in the deep end. If something went wrong, I was taught to relax instead of panic.

When my daughter was learning to swim, I told her that she could swim—period. The depth of the water had no bearing on her ability to swim. I explained that, at only 3 feet, 9 inches deep, even the shallow end of the pool was over her head. Therefore, if she could swim in a pool that was 4 feet deep, she could swim in an ocean that was 20,000 leagues deep. I do realize that there are always serious issues to consider when learning a skill that can potentially harm the student if she does not succeed at the task. What I am suggesting is that we let the student swim in the deep end with supervision. The security of supervision allows her to build confidence when she succeeds.

The learning process for selling is similar in many ways. In a number of our sales training classes, we teach a section called "Fear of the C-Level Call." Many sales people have never called on this "deep end" of an organization and, therefore, have developed a fear of making sales calls in the C-Suite. They are very comfortable calling on the first or second line manager in the organization but the thought of calling anyone higher is terrifying. This fear is unnecessary and unproductive.

But the real question is, why is this the case? It has a great deal to do with pressure. The Bing online dictionary defines pressure as "the constant state of worry and urgency." I have a different definition. I believe a person feels pressure when the imagined consequences of an act outweigh the positive possible outcomes of the act. For example, when Brittany was swimming across the pool in the shallow end, she focused on the technique of her strokes, breathing and kicks. She was free to think of nothing else because she knew she could stand on the bottom with her head above water if necessary. This type of concentration leads to a much greater chance for success. However, when she was swimming across the deep end, she'd been taught that this act could have dangerous consequences. This type of teaching is a mistake. The swim across the pool was no bigger or longer in the deep end.

Many sales professionals are taught the same thing about calling on an organization. The first line manager call is routine and there is nothing to fear. There is no pre-call plan developed and preparation is not stressed because the salesperson has made dozens of these calls. (This topic is discussed further in Chapter 7.) The calls become routine and comfortable, so the salesperson does not need to keep her skills sharp. Often this lack of preparation is not recognized because the desired sales objective is reached based solely on strong client relationship. (Many weak salespeople have had extremely overblown results because of strong client relationships. Now I'm the last person to diminish the value of developing strong customer relationships, but I have seen many successful reps exposed when their environment is changed.)

So what happens when the opportunity developed with the first line manager leads to a C-Level call with Mr. Bossypants? The pressure is on. Why? There are two reasons for this. First, you've been taught that these calls are life and death, hire or fire. Secondly, it might have been awhile since you actually *prepared* a pre-call plan to reach the desired call objective. Suddenly, you've been thrown in the deep end and lack the confidence to swim. This is a very scary thought.

One technique that I teach to control this type of fear is to use a pre-shot routine. A pre-shot routine is a repeatable positive exercise used to produce a repeatable positive outcome. It is designed to minimize the impact of the moment so that you can focus on the act. Remember, my definition of pressure results when you focus on a potential negative outcome. This unrealistically amplifies the moment.

Perhaps the best example of exaggerating the moment is illustrated with the tightrope exercise. If I offer you five dollars to walk across the floor along a straight line, you will accept the challenge because it is easy and safe. But, if you imagine that line spanning across the Grand Canyon, you will turn me down flat. Your natural instincts force you to focus on the likely negative outcome of falling to your death.

[The best example of a pre-shot routine is displayed during a golf match. You may have noticed while watching the PGA on TV, that each golf pro repeats a series of motions before every swing. It starts with a few practice swings. Next, he stands behind the ball and visualizes the shot. Then he sets up, shuffling his feet just millimeters to the right stance. Finally, he swings. The routine is faithfully executed before every shot. A study of the brain activity shows that golf pros have high brain activity before they set up to hit the ball and almost no brain activity during the swing itself. Interestingly, amateur golfers have the complete opposite brain activity. Their heads become so cluttered with thoughts and anxiety that they cannot execute a successful shot.]

Pressure does not have to cause angst in order to have a negative impact. I learned this while playing high school basketball. As a junior, I was chosen to take the last shot in a game. We were down by one point with 10 seconds left. During the timeout, our coach drew up a play for me. I was pumped, ready and not a bit nervous.

I'll elevate higher and follow through better than during the other shots I've made so far, I thought. Everything went as planned until the shot. I leaped higher than normal, extended my arm further, and the ball went sailing clear over the rim. I had overemphasized the moment by trying too hard and the adrenaline rush I experienced didn't help either. Up until that point in the game, I had made three consecutive 18-foot jump shots because I had stayed within the natural flow of the game. Like a golf pro setting up to swing, I only had to repeat my motions in the same automatic way. But even though I wasn't fearful, the idea of having to make the game-winning shot amplified my ambitions and disrupted my focus.

When faced with closing the Billion-Dollar Deal, the Consultative Selling approach was the same as it would have been for a million-dollar deal, a hundred-thousand dollar deal, or a hundred-dollar deal. My challenge was to control the external factors and the people from IBM and DialTex who risked overshooting the hoop by overemphasizing the moment.

Our sales blueprint controls us. Some salespeople are comfortable selling small deals but, as the tightrope elevates and the numbers get bigger, they find it difficult to walk across it. Top salespeople never fear the big deals. We embrace them. Instead, we fear the people who fear the big deals. No matter the profession, if you're working with a colleague who can't handle the moment, their fear will impact your performance, too. That is why an assessment of a person's Attitude and Intelligence is so important when building a sales team. I'm not talking about an assessment test. It's far more beneficial to talk to someone's peers and watch how the candidate performs in action than to review a personality test. Sales is a results business. You either achieve quota or you don't. It's pass or fail.

In professional sports, there are three types of top performers:
- Players who perform well in the regular season but struggle in the playoffs.
- Players whose performance is steady regardless of the situation. Derek Jeter falls into this category.
- Players who take their performances to an even higher level during crunch time. Michael Jordan, Tiger Woods, and Joe Montana are examples of this level of greatness.

Your performance category will depend on your ability to control the moment while under pressure, and the pre-shot routine will be your friend. As gifted as we are, our human brains can only focus on one thing at a time. If you can stay in the moment and focus on your pre-shot routine, your results under pressure will look just like your regular season performance. Please note that I did not say that you would perform *better* under pressure. That type of greatness is not learned; it's a gift.

How do you overcome this fear? You start by developing a routine to prepare for these calls now. Every time you make a sales call, it should be preceded by a pre-call plan. Continuing to develop your sales techniques will result in confidence in any situation. Your calls on first line managers are very important. If approached properly, you will find that you can discuss last night's big game as well as the impact of a recent news article on your client's business. No matter how strong your relationship, you should always try to add business value every time you reach out to your customer. This level of preparation will earn you the right to call at the next level. Your client's objective will be aligned with yours because this move could help him strengthen a relationship at the next level as well.

As a result, your call on Bossypants will be no different from any other call in that account. You will have been studying the client's business for months and will understand the requirements. You will have had several discussions with Bossypants' staff regarding his initiatives and how your solution can help. You've been ready for this call for a while. All you need to do is fine tune the impact of any current company news and determine if any of Bossypants' personal details are relevant to the call.

Let's discuss the depth of water you'll be swimming in. Just as Brittany used the same depth while swimming in either end of the pool, you will be doing the same. One of the most common mistakes reps make in these calls is assuming that the CFO wants you to come in and be his CFO peer. But beware: he doesn't want you to tell him how to run his business! In fact, if you really want to upset a C-Level executive in your next call, try to demonstrate how prepared you are to *be him*. I assure you, it will be a short call. You can't be his peer, so do not even try to go that deep. He simply wants you to be the sales professional who understands his business and is an expert on how your product or service will help him achieve his business objectives.

By the way, the first line manager you regularly call on expects the same thing. The biggest difference in these calls is that the C-Level executive doesn't have as much time so you might have to swim a bit faster. Therefore, once you've met your call objective, get out. If you can save him some time, he will appreciate it and be more likely to give you another opportunity. Remember, a C-Level executive is not looking for a friend. He is looking for a solution to a business problem. When you've earned the right to take the relationship to the next level, he will let you know.

5
THE LAYOFF

One of the things people often forget is that large deals like DialTex can consume you. You can work 24/7 and still get asked for more. I had other pressing matters in my unit. For example, there was a layoff. I had to let go of two employees, including a friend, Clark Honeycutt. Everyone liked Clark and I had saved his job twice before. Clark's customers loved him, but his skill set was average. He often required help in areas where other salespeople on his level didn't. He was one of four reps that I had directly reporting to me because I could protect him easier that way. But Clark's luck had run out and I had no choice but to let him go.

I had laid off dozens of people before, but Clark would be different. We shared a unique bond—cancer. My mother died of the awful disease and Clark was recovering from brain cancer so, for several years, we had shared, consoled and encouraged each other. The toll cancer takes on the stricken and their families is unfathomable. But the strength cancer patients possess is inspirational and Clark was no different. Fortunately, he had been in remission for well over a year, but that didn't make my directive any easier.

The day we announced who would be laid off was also the day I had to present my quarterly review and gap plan. This review, like all others that year, would be heavily focused on the DialTex deal. I would have to be sharp, focused and unencumbered by any ancillary duties. But the stress of terminating two employees—especially a friend—would prove difficult to suppress that day.

Corporate executives are required to suppress emotions and remain calm in the storm to such a degree that many of us short circuit. That's why I preach balance in these situations. Stress in ... stress out. If we can't balance stress, nature does it for us, often resulting in ulcers, heart disease, depression, alcohol and drug abuse, and countless other maladies. The number of my close colleagues who have suffered through chemical dependency or divorce is staggering. In fact, I have two close friends—both former corporate executives—whose stress-related problems led them to incarceration. And I'm not talking about hardened criminals. They served on nonprofit boards, belonged to the Country Club, and had kids in Ivy League schools. Watching these precipitous falls is surreal. It's like watching a movie because there is nothing they will let you do to help. That's why, in my training classes, I teach students how to "see the stress they possess."

My prescription is to engage in some type of physical exercise such as tennis, running, walking, weightlifting, golf, handball or any other activity. The important thing is to exercise regularly and with the same passion and intensity as the activities that are causing the stress. In other words, if you are an absolute loon at work, then you have to be the same loon while working out. This is the balance that will keep you healthy, strong and will provide a sustainable corporate career.

During the DialTex deal, I made sure that Hardy and the team took time to get away from work for brief periods. Hardy coached his son's baseball team and only missed two games during the deal. After a practice or game, he would return to work refreshed and work late into the evening. Coaching was Hardy's balance and I accepted the extra responsibility to ensure he achieved it.

This intensely stressful day would start with the layoffs, of which I now had two. The first was Clark and the second was Teddy Shifflet. I had been very dissatisfied with Teddy's performance, but I lost the fight to make his exit a firing because Human Resources thought a layoff would be easier. Both were in Washington, D.C., and I arrived the night before so I could relay the news in person first thing in the morning.

Teddy was supposed to be the first of the day. He had been a problem since before I took over the unit. It got so bad that a CIO actually had to call me after a mainframe win to explain that he had done nothing to help close the deal. She was buying the $4 million mainframe based on the good work of my large systems sales representative, not Teddy! This was indicative of Teddy's performance shortfalls and the reason why he was put on a Performance Improvement Plan months earlier.

Every time I'm in one of these situations, I recall a lecture from my Sales Management class in college. Dr. Miracle stood in front of the class and proclaimed, "Before teaching, I was a manager in corporate America for 20 years and I never fired anyone." After a long dramatic pause he continued, "They all fired themselves!" This certainly was the case with Teddy.

I didn't like or respect Teddy. I thought he was "stealing money" and should have been fired years earlier. However, at IBM, firings were difficult and took time. Layoff schedules occurred frequently enough to accommodate all of the employees like Teddy and then some.

As manager, I made sure every employee clearly understood his or her job duties. I regularly appraised their work and informed them when they were missing their mark. Then, in their Performance Improvement Plan, I explained what was needed to meet requirements and how long they had to complete them. Finally, I provided written communication that explained the consequences of the employee's failure to meet the requirements by the specified dates. Therefore, if the manager has done his or her job effectively, there are no surprises. If the employee elects not to comply, then they have sealed their own fate and fired themselves.

During layoffs at IBM, managers must follow a strict procedure that has been implemented by HR. If this procedure is not followed, it can expose the company to the risk of a labor suit. First, we were instructed not to apologize in any way. Saying "I'm sorry to inform you that you are on the list" is taboo. It could provide a chink in the company's armor that a decent labor attorney could easily penetrate. We had to robotically follow the script of the announcement and then move on to discussing the employee's benefits, severance and IBM's support services. It was a cold, clinical process.

That morning, I rescheduled the appointments so that Clark would be first because I believe in getting the tough stuff done as soon as possible. Then I could easily coast through Teddy's session with the requisite lack of feelings and emotion. Although I'm required to communicate everyone's fate to them, invariably, the ones on the list always know. IBM layoffs were based on ranking, and employees in Corporate America know how they are ranked even if the don't agree with their position.

When Clark walked in and sat down, I immediately recited the script. I was beginning to cover the benefits transition phase when he stopped me. "I thought that was going to be my news, but I have some news for you, too. Last week my doctor told me that my last scan showed another spot on my brain. My cancer is back."

My thoughts must have been transparent because he asked, "Are you okay? You don't look so good." Here was Clark—facing possible death, out of a job, and with a medical problem that would make finding a new one almost impossible—asking me if I was all right! His true character shone even more in tragedy than in success. Clark was a very good person who'd been dealt a very bad hand.

I was stunned, and I realized that my face must have gone blank. It took me a moment to gather myself. "Don't worry about me, I'm so sorry this layoff had to happen to you, especially now. I did everything I could to protect you, I feel just awful about this." I suddenly realized that I had let my feelings get the best of me. I had just broken every HR rule in the book. I also realized that I just didn't care about rules right now, I wanted to help a friend. We spent another hour behind closed doors breaking all of the other rules I might have missed.

I was now behind schedule, but at least this next termination wouldn't stress me out like the first—or so I thought. I quickly called my other employees to reassure them that they were not on the layoff list and was only 15 minutes late for Teddy. Of course he was also running late. Only Teddy could be 30 minutes late for his layoff meeting! When he walked in my office, I was stunned. It was 60 degrees outside and he wore a full-length trench coat buttoned to his neck. His face was flushed and he was sweating. Time stood still. My thoughts flashed to the postal worker who had shot his boss and a few colleagues during a layoff. But was I overreacting? Teddy didn't have a gun under his coat, did he? *Of course not*, I reassured myself. Just as I was beginning to calm down, I realized that every workplace shooting must have begun with someone saying, "No, not him."

I stood up, walked over and said, "Are you hot? Take your coat off and relax." With my hands, I patted him on both sides of his waist and joked, "You're not putting on weight, are you?" I didn't feel him concealing anything so I felt better. He unbuttoned his coat and sat down. I got right to it and made the announcement.

When I was done he said, "I thought that was the case. Look, can you give me a second to go to the bathroom? I rushed in here because I was late."

"Sure, I'll wait here," I said but, again, my mind raced. What if he came back blasting? Could it be possible that one employee told me he was facing death and the other wanted me to face a similar fate?

There were procedures in place for managers who felt threatened, but I would have felt like a wimp if I called security and there was no real threat. So I did the manly thing and ran. I dashed around to the opposite side of the bathroom and waited for him to come out. From my vantage point, he would exit the bathroom and turn away from where I was standing. I could follow him from behind and if he pulled a gun I could react. In that surreal moment, I felt as foolish as I did frightened.

Teddy was unstable but had never been violent. It was long rumored that he had a bad drinking and drug problem, but I never saw any evidence of this. He often seemed down. He once went missing in action for a couple of days and, when he returned, claimed he'd been sick with the flu. *Would it be far fetched for a drugged out and depressed sales representative to go postal on his manager after being laid off?* I reasoned. *Wilder things have happened with less provocation.*

When Teddy came out of the bathroom, I closely followed him. He moved slowly and seemed upset, but why shouldn't he? He had just been laid off. Before he turned away, I could see that his face was dry and his hair had been combed. That was a good sign. I don't believe people worry about their appearance before shooting their manager. However, he still had the trench coat on and I couldn't tell from behind if it was buttoned up. I followed him as he walked back to my office. He didn't stop or talk to anyone. I wanted to be close enough to him to see his initial reaction when approaching and entering my office. When Teddy got there, he walked in and made no sudden moves. I felt better but I still didn't like the coat.

I walked in behind him and said. "There you are. I needed a drink of water. Here, let me take your coat." I reached out to grab it from behind by the collar, which was awkward and out of character for me. Teddy turned and looked at me in surprise, then paused and gently smiled. It was as if he suddenly realized how the scene appeared to me.

"No worries," he replied and placed his coat on the adjacent chair.

My hands shook as my anxiety level came down and we finished the termination process without incident.

"Shoot," I said to myself, realizing that my day was so backed up now that my review was supposed to start in five minutes. I normally like to go over my slides one last time before they're opened up in front of senior management.

My anxiety level skyrocketed again and I couldn't wait to get back to the DialTex deal.

On the call was my VP, Scott Toms, who ran the east coast and his boss, Jerry Dork, the VP of the Americas. The review began with a question from Jerry, "Your two go okay?" I paused as the events of the day flashed through my mind. They were truly just numbers to him. It was hard to believe that a company who once had a full employment practice and was governed by "respect for the individual," was now run by managers who only cared to know that Clark and Teddy were terminated and that there was no risk of a labor suit. That's what Jerry meant by "okay". There would be no emotional support for having to layoff a friend. And there would be no indication from me that I couldn't handle the situation. Periodic layoffs were the hand we were now dealt at IBM. It was understood that we would man up and run our business. But fighting the disillusionment of regular layoffs on top of navigating The Billion Dollar Deal and my other accounts was a tall order.

"Yeah, they went fine," I casually said.

When two levels of management are on the call, it means that either your manager is in trouble or your territory is important. Since everyone south of Armonk knew about the DialTex deal, I assumed it was the latter. After I was poked and prodded from every angle, Scott let something slip. Don Tremble, a peer from IBM Global Services, had alluded to the fact that we were not running a tight ship. These kind of back-handed comments happened frequently. Sometimes, when being pressured in a review, a colleague cracks. He might need to set the stage so that a potential failure is not viewed as his alone. The account team is an easy target because we control everything. Every touch point between IBM and the customer is our responsibility. The support organizations will come and go depending on what the customer was buying and, in this case, DialTex was buying services.

In his review, Don could have questioned the strength of our relationships, customer satisfaction rating, access to decision makers, or a hundred other things. I pushed back, "If there is a specific concern that IBM Global Services has with how this deal is being run, let's discuss it."

Scott backed off, "It's probably nothing."

He was actually doing me a favor because he wanted me to know what Don had said. He also wanted me to handle Don. If he told me offline, he would be going behind his manager's back and I couldn't use the information to confront Don. However, by slipping and mentioning Don's disparagement in front of his manager, Scott was free from blame. He also wanted Don put in his place and knew I would do it.

IBM Global Services was setting us up. If we won the deal, they would claim that they saved us. If we lost the deal, it was our fault. I was being played. I realized what Scott was doing, but squashing Don would help us all and I was the man for the job.

In Corporate America, the game is never fair. The stakes are high and this sometimes breeds backstabbing, plagiarism and lies. The pressure causes people to crack in different ways. During a stressful inquisition, some will frantically say anything to get management off their backs. Later, they will apologize for throwing you under the bus. This weakness can be forgiven, but there are those with far more calculating tactics. Their goal is to win at your expense, which could be part of a larger scheme to steal your job.

I recall an incident early in my sales career. I had just qualified as a sales representative after a grueling fourteen months of sales training. I was assigned to a team account with a senior sales representative, but I also received my very own IBM account: Forefront. I knew IBM didn't give new salespeople the top accounts—for obvious reasons—but I didn't expect one as bad as Forefront. Forefront was a small mutual fund company that IBM had abandoned after they made a decision to go with Amdahl, our fiercest mainframe competitor. In those days, it was common for IBM to pull out of small accounts that made competitive decisions. This meant that we would have no sales, technical or service support on site. In other words, don't bother calling because we won't answer. We used to be so powerful that pulling out was used to teach customers a lesson. We would justify it by saying that IBM couldn't afford to provide dedicated support to customers who didn't have a substantial install base of IBM equipment. This was only partially true because we did it all of the time to many accounts as an investment for future business.

For one year, I worked hard, in addition to getting very lucky, and turned Forefront into a very big IBM customer. A few of the senior reps, who wouldn't have been caught dead at Forefront a year before, were telling management that I couldn't handle it. It would be risky to have so much revenue exposed to a rookie they said. I was devising a plan to defend my turf, when, surprisingly, I discovered that management fully supported me.

My manager, Bob McKeg, called me into his office and said, "Driscoll and Luff have each asked for Forefront."

"What? No! That's mine!"

"Relax, I told them no but they'll be watching and waiting for you to slip up. I fully support what you have done there. If you keep it up, this could be your ticket to whatever you want to do next at IBM."

I felt great! His support meant a lot to me. At the next branch meeting, I received my first Regional Manager's Award, which included a marble pen desk set and $7,500.

Now Scott was supporting me in a much different manner. The next day, I went to see Don in his office and firmly said, "I heard what you said about DialTex. If you ever try to disparage me or my team to management during this deal again, I will kick you off this account and make sure you don't work in my territory again."

He attempted a reply, but I cut him off and shut him down. When handling someone, you have to take the power and maintain complete control, so I didn't even let him speak. It was not a discussion—it was an order. Once I was certain he'd heard me, I quickly used Sam Sheepdog transitioning and calmly launched into a discussion about YellowPic, a call center partner for DialTex's west coast operations. It took him a minute to catch up to the discussion. He wasn't sure I had moved on and just stared at me for a second.

I repeated the question. "Where are we with YellowPic? Is their solution going to fully integrate with the others?"

"Uh, yes. It looks like it will, but it needs to be

tested with the volumes we are proposing for DialTex. My guys have started the testing today and we should know in two days."

I later found out that my quick transitions were the reason I was sometimes called Michael Jeckle.

ARE YOU LUCKY?

Whenever one of Napoleon's lieutenants recommended an officer for promotion, Napoleon would ask, "Is he lucky?" At first this would baffle the lieutenant because he had just finished extolling the many accomplishments of the officer, all of which qualified him for promotion. What does luck have to do with it? It turns out, a great deal. Many of the greats in sports, entertainment and business consider themselves lucky.

For example, in the beginning of actor Harrison Ford's career, things were not going very well. He supported himself as a carpenter while he struggled to become an actor. His lucky break came when a young director named George Lucas hired Ford to install some cabinets in his home and, as a result, he got an opportunity to audition for Lucas' next film. A year later, another young director, Francis Ford Coppola, hired Ford to expand his office. Coppola cast him in his Oscar-nominated thriller "The Conversation." Lucas later cast Ford in the role of Han Solo in "Star Wars," launching his legendary career. Ford may not have been the only carpenter these two great directors hired, but he was lucky to be the right one at the right time.

Rosario Dawson was discovered on her dad's front porch, and Charlize Theron was discovered in a bank trying to cash a check. The person who discovered each of them saw other people that day. The point is, luck brings opportunity. Talent, work ethic, preparedness and confidence close the deal. I believe that most of us have the same number of opportunities in life. Being ready to seize the moment is what separates the winners from everyone else.

I once overheard two IBM sales reps talking in an elevator. One was explaining how lucky he had been to recognize his customer's CIO when they rode the elevator together in the customer's building. For an IT sales person, the CIO is top dog because she is responsible for every decision relevant to the deal. But the rep went on to tell his colleague that he was "lucky" to see the CIO before being noticed so he was able to duck behind another person on the elevator and not be seen. He had met her once before with the lead rep but was horrified at the thought of having a conversation with her alone. If this rep had been prepared and confident, this chance meeting could have been the opportunity that changed his career.

There are so many stories about people being ready for the big moment. One of my favorites is Chesley "Sully" Sullenberger, the pilot who safely guided the plane into the Hudson River. When asked to describe his courage and calmness under fire, he said he had prepared himself for that moment his entire career.

As sales professionals, we have to prepare the same way. In our Water Institute Sales Training, we teach a section on the Elevator Pitch—that 30-second soundbite that fully describes the benefits of your offering. Depending on your area of sales, you might have several

Elevator Pitches. However, seizing your opportunities requires much more than an Elevator Pitch. Within every company, there are always one or two people who inexplicably seem to get the best account or promotion. They don't appear to be more talented, and seem almost average. However, they speak up ad nauseam, asking for more work and just annoying the heck out of everyone else. They may not be the best presenters, but they're the first to offer to present at the next branch meeting. As a builder of sales teams, I always chose the confident hard worker who was good over the supremely gifted person that rested on his laurels. The gifted ones usually won a higher percentage of deals, but hard workers got in front of more opportunities and produced more revenue with a lower closing rate. They are the ones who just happen to be at the right place at the right time and seem to produce a higher number of positive outcomes. Lucky? Louis Pasteur said, "Luck favors the prepared."

For me personally, there has been a great deal of good luck around all of my success in sales. Earlier in this chapter, I briefly discussed my success with Forefront, the innovative mutual fund company. When IBM pulled out of that account, the relationship was severed. Normally, this is a public "dissing" that officially ends the relationship unless the customer comes crawling back to IBM. But in Forefront's case, that was never going to happen. Their management team was bright, strong-willed and unforgiving. When I qualified as a new IBM sales rep, I was given Forefront as my new solo account because it was a low-risk proposition. I couldn't screw up an account that already hated IBM.

So there I was on my first call with the CIO. I had a clue that this was going to be an uphill battle when he said, "I only agreed to meet with you because I wanted to be able to tell you face-to-face that I will never buy anything from IBM again!" I suddenly remembered hearing that the last meeting between IBM and Forefront ended with him and our branch manager engaged in a shouting match.

I had to diffuse this deep-rooted anger. "Oh, I know that," I said casually. "I heard about the history between our two companies, most of which happened when I was in college. I'm a brand new sales rep, so we both know why I was given this account. I have no plans to try and sell you anything. But, you are currently running IBM software on your Amdahl mainframe. You still have some of our tape and disk storage machines. Since IBM service and support people are working here daily, I just want to ensure that at least this part of our relationship goes well."

"You certainly won't make any money doing that," he said with a wry smile. I could see that he was enjoying my pain.

He wouldn't enjoy it for long though, because I was about to get lucky, and I was prepared.

"True. But this is the hand I've been dealt and I'm just trying to do the best with it," I answered him. "But, in return, I do ask one favor: I would like you to judge me, not IBM, moving forward. I was in freshman English when all of this went down. I didn't cause it, nor can I erase what happened."

"You got that right, but you'll have to live with it!" he said emphatically.

When I had first walked into his office, I noticed a picture of him completing a local 5K run. I had also run that event a couple of times. A CS always scans a client's office for clues to what makes a client tick. Since offices are usually decorated with items of fondness, if he had a picture of himself finishing that 5K, then he was proud of it. It was low-hanging fruit.

As I was getting up to leave, I pointed to the picture and asked, "So what was your time?"

"What?" he replied, caught off guard. "Uh, 19:22." That meant he had paced about a 6-minute mile. Not bad. This was my opening. I had several friends who were runners—world-class runners. If running was his passion, this might be my lucky break.

"I couldn't break 20, but came close." I said dismissively. This was perfect! I was good enough to be credible, but not faster than him. "But my buddy, Ray, ran a 16:50."

"Ray who?" he grilled.

"Ray Brown. He also won the 800 at the U.S. National Indoor Championship six years in a row."

"You know Ray Brown?"

"Yeah, he's a college buddy of mine. Ray has introduced me to a bunch of track guys."

I spent the next 20 minutes namedropping. I later found out that there was a running culture at Forefront. Many employees competed in 5Ks, 10Ks and even marathons. There was a lunchtime running club and several of my clients ran the company course daily.

When acknowledging a picture or other ornament in a client's office, I suggest taking it slowly—you don't want to appear too transparent. You have to earn the right to move the discussion from the current business topic. Start with a business reference such as a plaque on the wall recognizing a company achievement. This is usually innocuous and permitted even in the first meeting. But in my case with the Forefront client, I had nothing more to lose.

The CIO and I developed a good relationship. He never liked IBM and often criticized the company, not me, for everything. My good luck continued when the mutual fund industry exploded in the mid 1990s. Forefront's business grew by double digits annually. We won back the mainframe and sold them every IBM hardware platform, multiple IBM services and OS/2 and Lotus Notes. OS/2 was our PC operating system that competed with Windows. Today, 15 years later, Forefront is one of IBM's largest OS/2 customers. There are very few left.

When I started on the account, Forefront had about 2,500 employees and their assets totaled about $50 billion. When I left the account, they had more than 14,000 employees and had assets of more than $500 billion. Three of my four Golden Circle sales awards—won for achieving top two percent worldwide--came from my success at Forefront. I had been lucky, and I was prepared.

Obviously, this situation could have turned out drastically differently. If I had taken into the account all of the negative energy I had received from my peers, I surely would have failed. "I heard you got Forefront. My condolences," they jibbed when I was assigned the account. When I met the CIO, I could have tucked my tail and run away, but I challenged him. A successful CS will often challenge the client. You are there to add value to the client's business. If you come across as weak or unsure, this will crush your credibility. And, as Tab Edwards says, "Credibility is the most important thing a CS can have."

So I remained positive, challenged the customer, provided the best customer service that I could and ultimately earned the right to compete for Forefront's business. The fact that circumstances beyond my control caused Forefront's business to grow by leaps and bounds in six years was fortuitous. All I could do was prepare the environment to receive this good fortune.

6
THE TRICKS AND THE TRAITOR

As a CS, one of the benefits of strong customer relationships is that you have earned some degree of good will with your clients. Throughout the course of your time with them, they may have made mistakes that you've covered up or there may have been budgetary constraints you've accommodated by waiving fees or not charging for certain services. One such relationship of mine saved us during the Dialtex deal.

"What do you mean it's not shipping this quarter?!" I shouted.

A month before we embarked on the Billion-Dollar Deal, a large, competitive mainframe deal stalled on us. We had won the deal, but our customer could not accept delivery at the time because the board had yet to put their rubber stamp of approval on it. This happens often, but as long as you understand the client's approval process, you can plan for such delays. So often I see salespeople assume that they and their client are aware of every step of the approval process within the client's company. For transactions under a certain dollar amount, approvals don't require board approval but, over a certain threshold, they do. And there are other criteria of a deal that, if missed, can kill or delay opportunities. Services deals are sometimes viewed differently than hardware deals. As we will discuss later, the most difficult services deal to get approved is an outsourcing deal. Due to the inherent risk involved, outsourcing deals face more scrutiny no matter their size, simply because the customer is giving up control.

In the case of our mainframe deal, my team had accounted for the required board approval, but the board meeting had been postponed because a key member was ill. I had accepted the risk and forecasted this transaction. I had personally worked on the deal because it had been my account when I was a sales rep. As a result, I knew all the players and my relationships with them were very strong.

So it wasn't one of my reps or managers on the hook for this one—it was me. This was an $8 million competitive win against Hitachi. Management had already celebrated it. I had approved a branch manager's award for the sales representative and was scheduled to present it at our next branch meeting. I didn't want anything to mar this deal. Any mistakes could raise doubt that I could pull off the DialTex deal. I had to fix it. The box had to ship!

I reviewed the situation in my mind:

- The deal was won and approved by the CIO.
- The board had to grant a perfunctory approval.
- The board has never reversed the CIO's approval.
- The box was scheduled to ship the next day.
- The customer legally couldn't accept delivery until board approval.
- IBM doesn't recognize revenue for the sale until the box ships.

One of the issues with shipping mainframes at that time was that they had to remain in a controlled environment. The temperature and humidity were regulated throughout its transport from the IBM plant to the customer's data center floor. In addition, it had to ship to the customer before IBM could take credit for the sale. Therefore, we couldn't simply ship the box to one of our warehouses and say it went to the customer.

Fortunately, one of my best accounts was located half a block away from this customer. If I could convince the CIO to receive the box on his loading dock, I could have another shipper pick it up and take it to our warehouse. After board approval, we could ship it to the customer. Risky, but it could work.

I called the CIO, who we will call John Doe, and asked him for a quick meeting. John was one of my first and favorite clients. We had worked, played and fought harder than any salesperson/client partnership I knew. I had covered for him during some difficult problems and he had bought everything IBM sold. John also chose not to nail me on a $100,000 mistake I made with his account early in my career. I had even yelled at him before, something our unique bond allowed me to do.

In his office, I explained my dilemma and asked for the favor. John was a colorful orator, telling me exactly what I could do with myself and calling me insane.

"How dare you ask me to take that risk?!" he barked.

He was upset that I would ask him to risk so much. The customer I was asking him to impersonate was highly visible. I had not considered John's risk. It wouldn't be just his risk personally but could also be viewed as a federal offense by his company. Knowing him as I did, I had to give John a moment to calm down. Then I could make another run at it, now understanding his objection.

He took a deep breath and calmly said, "So you want

me to intercept a multi-million dollar IBM asset that is officially going somewhere else, impersonate that company by signing as their CIO, take delivery on my loading dock, and then let another shipper pick it up and hide this multi-million dollar asset for two weeks?"

"Exactly," I confidently agreed as I looked him straight in the eye. As ridiculous as it sounded, I had to remain calm and cool as though I did this kind of thing all the time. "But let me explain. You're right that I had not fully considered your risk but, in a way, that's why I came to you. I know you know how to make this work. I believe we can come up with a way to do this without putting your company at risk. So do me this favor, let's talk through this situation objectively as if it is a case study. Let's not concern ourselves with whether or not we're going to do it yet. Let's just see if we can figure this puzzle out together."

The interesting thing about sales is that even when a client can see that you are playing him, if executed correctly, he is defenseless. I knew John loved crossword puzzles and we often discussed my business case studies when I was completing my certification at Harvard. John knew that I was using his passion to control him, but he couldn't resist the challenge. It took us about twenty minutes to construct the solution. The scenario would go as planned, with me assuming responsibility for the most egregious acts and ensuring that his alibi—he would claim he wasn't there at the time of delivery and knew nothing about the situation—was intact.

Whew! I left his office feeling on top of the world. Again, the best way to measure your value as a CS is not in dollars sold, but in the strength of your relationships. I knew 100 IBM reps who could have closed this tough competitive deal, but I could only think of maybe five who could have done what I had just done with John. I told the account rep who was patiently waiting in the lunchroom that it was done. She didn't need to know the details.

The next day, I was preparing to go pull off the caper on John's loading dock when I got a call from the actual customer. I picked up to find the CIO, Bill, on the phone, upset that our shipper was attempting to deliver the IBM mainframe on two semi-trucks!

Shoot, they were early! And they'd gone to the actual customer! I had to diffuse this situation fast. The last thing I needed was more attention on this deal. "Bill, there is obviously a mistake. Of course I know you can't receive the box yet. They must have mixed up the ship date at our plant. I'm ten minutes away. Hold tight and I'll be down to fix this right away."

On the way, I was kicking myself for not anticipating this problem. Although we had changed the ship-to address in the ordering system, it can take time for the change to take effect. Also, the shipper could have pulled and printed the customer information early, before we updated it. This is common because ship-to addresses for mainframes don't usually change. After all, it's not the kind of thing you can just ship anywhere.

I had to develop a plan on the way over. What did I know?

- Two semi-trucks were in the city, parked outside of the "wrong" customer's loading dock.

- They are fairly noticeable, so I had to assume that their IT staff also knew they were there.

- Getting those two large trucks to deliver the box

half a block away without being noticed by someone at the customer's location would be impossible.

- Having the shipper return the order to our plant would be a death sentence.

- I would have to act alone.

In a company as large as IBM, shipping mistakes happen all the time. Why couldn't this be a simple mistake? But then I would have to come up with a reason to deliver to John's facility. I considered many options, but the mistake angle won out. When I got to the customer, there were people from IT standing near the truck.

When they saw me, they all made jokes. "Hope you have a big house 'cause that ain't coming here!" someone shouted.

"I thought they stopped you from filling out order forms?" another jibed.

This was good. I could run with the mistake angle. I approached one driver alone and let him have it. "What in the world are you people doing? I just checked the system and this is not supposed to come here!"

I explained how dissatisfied I was with his company and was going to let management know that he had screwed up big-time. I told him to call dispatch ASAP and check the delivery address. He did and confirmed the mistake. I went on to explain that I hate looking bad in front of my customer so we had to fix this quietly. He got on the phone, radioed the other driver and they left for the "correct" location. I confirmed with the IT manager that the problem had been resolved and he agreed to update Bill. I then walked the half block to John's loading dock and found his receiving manager waiting. When the trucks arrived, I had to play traffic cop and direct cars to wait as these two mammoth trucks backed up to the dock.

The other two semis I was using to transport the box to our warehouse arrived shortly after we did. This created an absolute traffic nightmare on a Friday afternoon in the downtown part of the city. I had to direct traffic again and several employees from both companies saw me and greeted me with more jokes as they returned from lunch. I then realized that even if I were able to pull this off without getting fired or going to jail, I wouldn't live this down for a long time. One thing that would help them believe the "mistake" angle is that, as a sales representative, I had the reputation for doing whatever was necessary for my customers. They had seen me get my hands (and suit) dirty on more than one occasion. Although quite funny, seeing me play traffic cop in an Armani suit was not as unusual as you might expect.

The box was delivered to the dock, inventoried, signed for, loaded by the other shipper and then taken away. As he was leaving, the driver for the first shipper that I had just berated gave me a long, knowing look as he got back into his truck.

I climbed up into his cab window, gave him a wink, put $60 in his hand and said, "Thanks."

"Don't mention it," he replied with a hearty laugh and drove away.

Surprisingly, only a few customers asked about the weird delivery. I explained that I was unhappy with the first shipper and didn't want them to have responsibility for the box any longer.

The next few weeks at DialTex went as smoothly as could be expected with this type of deal. We had our regular fires to put out with pricing, solution design and business partner issues, but that was business as usual.

Then came our next team checkpoint meeting. These were very productive meetings where everyone involved gathered in a big conference room or on a conference call and discussed every detail of the deal. Every deadline, customer issue and action item was reviewed ad nauseam. Being a process guy, I loved these meetings. They helped me know who was doing his or her job, who wasn't, and where we needed help. This reduced surprises and helped me sleep better at night. After all, I couldn't fix what I didn't know about. Before the meeting began, there was a great deal more chatter than normal. Something was up and it was either very good or very bad. I approached four of my colleagues who were huddled together and asked, "What's up?"

Someone on the other side of the room heard my question and quickly chimed in, "John Buchannan jumped ship!"

"Where?!" I demanded in disbelief.

"GDS."

"That son of a ... gun." I said in a more subdued voice. "Are you freaking kidding me?" Then I was silent.

My wife has always said that she can tell when I am really mad because I get unusually quiet. I'm quiet because I'm concocting some of the vilest forms of retaliation possible.

Buchannan was a shock. He had been a work friend for several years. He'd started a few years before me and was one of the reps that helped me during my sales training. Later, he had an area staff position where he specialized in large systems marketing, and we closed a lot of big iron together. It was out of character for him to be the one jumping ship for our fiercest outsourcing rival in the middle of a deal. I had seen this happen a few times over the years and a person making such a Benedict Arnold move burns every bridge they have ever crossed. There's no going back.

We spent the entire meeting in damage control. Buchannan had been in a position at IBM Global Services to know enough about the deal to cripple us. I asked everyone in the room to briefly detail what sensitive information they had e-mailed, discussed or physically given him in the last month. We determined that our deal had changed to such a degree over the previous month that anything older would have been obsolete.

We got halfway through this exercise when we realized that we didn't need to continue. Buchannan had prepared for this. He had enough to hurt us. Of course we had non-compete clauses in all employee contracts, but they weren't as bulletproof then as they are now. Moreover, IBM didn't go to great lengths to enforce these agreements. Most of our non-competing agreements didn't prevent employees from leaving for a competitor in the same industry. They didn't even restrict them from working in a particular geographical area. After all, IBM is a multinational company with a presence just about everywhere. At the time, the non-compete agreements only prevented employees from going to a competitor and calling on his or her existing customer base for a period of time.

Most defectors circumvented this by working with a different set of customers and running important deals in their old territory from behind the scenes. They would construct deals with their new company to be officially or unofficially compensated for everything they helped close in their former IBM territory. Because this was easy to do and impossible to prove, IBM usually chose to ignore the betrayals.

I, however, couldn't overlook this kind of backstabbing. The previous two times it had happened to me, I went to my customers and appealed to their high moral standards, asking them to not let the rat win the deal. It worked both times.

However, this time was different. IBM couldn't let a key resource leave for our competitor with confidential information during a $1.2 billion deal without a fight. And fight we did.

The plan was to cry foul to the customer and try to get GDS disqualified from the deal. At the very least, we could expose the situation and receive some type of dispensation down the road. Of course, GDS denied to the customer that they would ever use confidential IBM information to gain an unfair competitive advantage. They told the customer they had placed Buchannan in an executive, non-sales capacity in another region. In that role, he would have no direct customer contact. But somehow this didn't make me feel any better.

It probably wasn't as bad as it looked on the surface, however. Our two companies had competed for so long that we knew each other's offerings as well as our own. It was likely that Buchannan had only validated a few things GDS already knew. It certainly didn't help for them to have our pricing, but nothing was final yet anyway. Moreover, although important, price would not be the deciding factor. We were both going to save DialTex money because the winner would be the company offering the best long-term solution to make them more efficient. And Buchannan wasn't on the short list of people I thought understood our overall strategy well enough to articulate it to the customer.

We had Jerry Dork make an emergency phone call to Tony Gaudenza, the COO of DialTex, and raise his concerns. This was a play to create as much exposure to the situation as possible. It could give us grounds to protest the deal if we lost. DialTex didn't want any negative press on this deal so they, in turn, went to GDS and expressed their concerns. Ultimately, Buchannan was fired because the risk of keeping him was too great.

Although he made out well financially in the settlement, I felt good knowing that Buchannan got what he deserved. I found out later that the top brass at GDS were not initially aware of Buchannan's hiring. It was the local management team that was dumb enough to think they could pull off the ill-advised stunt.

We had a few weeks before our proposal was due and, contrary to IBM Global Services' beliefs, the value of the account team would be clearly demonstrated as we moved forward.

WE'RE TALKING ABOUT PRACTICE

Most salespeople only practice when forced to do some type of sales training. We seem to approach it like basketball player Allen Iverson, whose classic rant regarding why he didn't need to practice was recently celebrated on ESPN replays.

The main reason some sales people don't like to practice sales calls and presentations with our peers is because it makes us feel uncomfortable. As my sales role model, Mike Forgash, told me, one of the most difficult things we have to overcome is being openly judged by our peers.

But I still find this puzzling. Most of us have a hobby or play a sport. Golfers will spend hours at the range trying to fix a slice. They are comfortable asking friends for feedback or making a video recording of their swing. They will also pay thousands of dollars to receive professional help. The same is true for those who play tennis or a musical instrument. Most salespeople I know should be far more embarrassed when demonstrating their backhand than their sales call techniques.

During our training classes, we promote a sales culture that openly practices together. We also do this internally at Marketing and Business Integration. For example, one of my partners routinely calls me on the phone and assigns me a random name. Instantly, I know that I am in character and he is rehearsing for an upcoming call. After the role play, we debrief and I give my feedback. He thinks catching me off guard makes for a more natural experience.

This type of regular practice is the fastest way to improve. I realize that it can be uncomfortable at first, but after a few weeks, you will actually look forward to it. If you've ever had your golf swing recorded, I'm sure you remember how surprised you were to see what it really looked like. There are so many unconscious mistakes we make that would never get corrected if we didn't see ourselves perform. When we play back video of a salesperson's training session presentation and he sees the change jingling in his pocket or notices how many times he says "Um," it immediately helps him self-correct. The bottom line is that we want to make our mistakes during practice and not in front of the customer.

Technology today has made video recording so easy that anyone with a Smartphone can do it. I challenge you to privately video yourself practicing a 5-minute presentation and see what involuntary habits you uncover. No one will have to know that you've done it, and I guarantee that it will generate positive results. If you are a manager, try to adopt a practicing culture in your organization. Some of the more seasoned salespeople will be the hardest to change so have them be the trainers. They can practice with the younger reps before sales calls. At least the next generation of your sales team will be accustomed to practicing and your organization will be better for it.

One important tool that salespeople need to practice is their Elevator Pitch. You need to be prepared in case you're lucky enough to run into that executive you've been trying to see for weeks. "Duh, uhmmm," is usually not going to get you a meeting. Don't practice memorization because a memorized script can come across sounding canned and doesn't allow you to key off of a response. But, you should be prepared to smoothly and confidently articulate a 30 – 60 second message naturally.

7
THE PROPOSAL

During the last few weeks before the proposal was due, we had our people flying in and out of DialTex like it was a beehive. Our technical people needed to ensure that our solution would support the customer. In the areas where we were allowed to make substitutions to their applications, we had to validate and discuss all of the recommendations with DialTex's technical teams to get buy in. The pace quickened. Our status meetings occurred more frequently. There were more conference calls, strategy sessions and internal meetings after hours and on weekends. Our deadline was July 31. People were interrupted at home and on vacation, but most postponed their vacations until after the due date. A deal like this one is a symphony that involves many movements and, as the deadline approaches, everything builds to an exploding crescendo. This deal would consume our lives until it was over.

We had now selected all of our partners for this deal. That meant both the winners and losers had to be notified. I'm sure you recall Dennis, my next-door neighbor, whose company was competing to partner with IBM on the call center business. They had a very good solution that was priced competitively because their call centers were in India. From Dennis, I learned about accent neutralization, which is when call center employees are trained to infer that they are located in the U.S. They have stage names like Bob or Nancy and imply they live in Ohio. "Boy, it's hot in Cincinnati today," one might say in an effort to make the caller feel like they were talking to someone stateside. Dennis told me of a survey that determined callers prefer to get help from someone located geographically close to them. Given a choice between two toll-free 24/7 support centers, callers far more frequently select the closer option. When you add a foreign country and the employee's accent into the equation, callers start off even more frustrated. Dennis explained that accent neutralization was designed to overcome these setbacks.

Nevertheless, we decided to buy American and selected a different call center partner. I asked to be the one to deliver the news to Dennis because I thought that I could soften the blow a bit. It was a delicate situation because Dennis had been working on the biggest opportunity of his career and he happened to be friends with a neighbor who had a fair amount of influence on the decision. As a

CS, you couldn't ask for a better situation and most would take those odds!

But that's why we teach that a deal is never done until the contracts are signed. Not to mention the fact that most of us have been in situations where we have lost a deal even after contract signature. Dennis actually took it pretty well. Still, it's never fun to be the bearer of bad news.

We delivered the proposal on time, although it wasn't one of those government deals where being late meant that you were dead. Over the next few weeks, the ball was in DialTex's court. They would review the proposal, develop questions and schedule orals, in which each respondent would present their recommendation to DialTex's decision team. This is also where the account team adds value. Because my team was in the account on a daily basis, we were commissioned to check with our contacts to glean any useful information. This was just another situation in which the services group relied upon us to deliver something they couldn't while giving us no credit. If we couldn't get good information, we were criticized for lack of account control. If we uncovered something that could give us a competitive advantage, it was business as usual.

Orals were scheduled two weeks out. This gave DialTex time to read all of the proposals and understand each offering. Then they could prepare questions for each potential vendor to answer during their presentations.

Because IBM and GDS knew a great deal about each other's offerings, we could tell what DialTex liked and disliked about the proposals based on the questions they asked. In our next status meeting, we combed through the questions and assigned members of the team to craft IBM responses to each question. Of course, Hardy and his team were asked to test some of our responses with their contacts in advance.

The account stayed busy. We continued to have new IBM colleagues calling on DialTex almost daily. Each person had to hear Hardy's admonishments of "Don't say this" and "Don't do that." Hardy and I were cut from the same cloth when it came to account control. Far too often, an executive or techie would call on an account and say the wrong thing and we were left to clean up the mess. As a CS, you should know more about the politics of your account than anyone.

On a number of occasions, I had to tell certain colleagues—even those with a higher pay grade— that they were not welcome in my account. This will never be easy for you as a CS, but remember, you're the one who lives there every day.

The people who drive decisions don't always carry the biggest title. Smart organizations rely more heavily upon smart people when faced with crucial choices. Sometimes these smart people are not interested in being CEO someday. They have a passion for their craft and want to be the best they can at it. In meetings, they sometimes don't look, act or sound like they have the power to influence anything. But an effective CS knows these people do have influence and will develop relationships with them.

In meetings, while the technical team is discussing the intricate details that make a solution work, the CS is reading the audience. We watch facial expressions, eye movement and other non-verbal communication. In the call debrief after the meeting, while the techies are engrossed in discussion of a configuration concern, the CS's are saying things like, "Did you see how the CIO looked at Jane in finance? She's the person making this decision." During my career, I have had a janitor, a cab driver, a security guard, a cafeteria worker and countless administrative assistants provide me with information that helped to close deals. Never underestimate someone's influence and never base their knowledge on their job title.

When we prep colleagues during the pre-call plan, they don't always listen. Corporate executives who are good at what they do often think they know more about an account than the salesperson. After all, many of them were successful sales reps at some point in their careers as well. However, like parents, they seem to have forgotten what they used to do all those years before.

This happened to Hardy on the DialTex deal. We had J.R. Winnfield, III coming in from our research center. He was as smart as he was pompous. I have seen a countless number of big egos at IBM, but few colleagues have reached J.R.'s level of brilliance and arrogance. He subscribed to Muhammad Ali's notion that "It ain't bragging if it's true." J.R. rarely made house calls. He usually only presented at the briefing center or at large IBM events. But this deal warranted his presence on site.

Hardy is not afraid to tell anyone the rules of his account, but J.R. didn't listen. The meeting was designed to have J.R. brief DialTex on a few key topics, present our five-year plan and spend the second half of the meeting leading a question-and-answer session. As usual, J.R. gave a spectacular presentation. Hardy could see that the group was completely absorbed in J.R.'s knowledge.

The tide turned quickly, however, during the question-and-answer time. John Rayburn, the Technical Services Manager, asked a question. As usual, John wore jeans and stood in sharp contrast to his suited-up colleagues.

"Why did you choose that design for this application?" he asked. Hardy thought it was nothing more than a question about personal preference. J.R. seemed to take it as a challenge to his knowledge.

"It's just how it's done," he retorted. "I've personally seen this design used all over the world," J.R. continued his condescension with a litany of examples as though John had asked a stupid question. John backed down.

After the call, J.R. bragged about how he had put John in his place at the same time that he ensured his approach was accepted by the real decision-makers. That was one of the meeting objectives and it was important to our solution. But at what cost?

Hardy knew that, while J.R. boasted, John was offended and could possibly fight our solution internally. Now Hardy had to clean up J.R.'s mess. As salespeople, we can sometimes win a battle but lose the war. I have always said, "There's no ego during the sale. Save it for the celebration." Once a deal has been won, there is plenty of time for self-praise. J.R.'s ego trip would come back to bite us at a critical time in the deal.

Orals are an interesting time because it's the point where all of your resources are utilized. Your best technical, financial, presentation and perception skills are tested to the fullest. Everyone is assigned a role. The pre-call plan is developed and rehearsed in excruciating detail. Nothing is left to chance. The tone of these meetings is very different from regular presentations because customers want to demonstrate that they are creating an equal playing field for all. Clients with whom you might have played golf yesterday will act like they just met you during orals. It's all part of the game.

GDS was scheduled to present first and then IBM. This was a great position because we would have the luxury of reading how DialTex viewed the GDS solution. The other two vendors were scheduled after us, but everyone knew it was between IBM and GDS.

I couldn't be there because we already had more people attending the meeting than DialTex wanted. Hardy's only speaking part was to kick things off in the introduction, so I was comfortable with him observing and updating me in real-time. This was before texting technology, so we used our two-way pagers to communicate during the meeting.

Everything went as planned through the Introduction, Solution Design and Pricing phases of the meeting. We were prepared and had properly addressed all of the questions that DialTex had submitted earlier. However, when it came to the open question-and-answer session, we hit a problem. This time, John Rayburn led that portion of the meeting. Hardy thought he had diffused the situation between him and J.R., but it soon became apparent that ill feelings remained.

John described how our approach in a particular area was different from the other vendors. He supported DialTex's approach with white paper references and examples from other large organizations using the same design. This was completely inappropriate for orals because the customer never presents, the vendors do. John was only supposed to facilitate the question-and-answer session. J.R. wasn't there so we had no one present who could even come close to engaging in a detailed technical discussion, let alone defend our position. John's message—through our team--to J.R. was clear: Don't screw with his baby and don't publicly embarrass him.

Hardy messaged me on my pager. "John is killing J.R. ... awkward... we can't defend ... won't stop!"

We had to diffuse this quickly! It wasn't going to kill our deal, but we didn't want negative press about our meeting spreading through DialTex.

"Understand, Empathize and Accept!" I instructed. Hardy would know what this meant. When in a public situation where a customer will not yield an inch, absolutely do not fight him even if you're 100% right and can prove it with a mound of supporting documentation. Because even if you win the argument, it will only embarrass the client and kill your relationship. So you have to lose without losing.

"Excuse me, John," Hardy politely interrupted. "I understand that your existing solution design for the hierarchical database is different from the one we have proposed for the design of your future state. This is such an important part of DialTex's operation and, since you designed and wrote it, we should spend more time ensuring that we get it right. If you'll agree, we can make the changes to our proposal and resubmit next week. Is that okay?"

John agreed.

The rest of the session went fine. After the meeting, our team had a debrief call in another one of DialTex's conference rooms. The services and technical teams were livid at Hardy for conceding the point. We needed to change the database because using our competing product would allow us to be cheaper.

However, we needed the change to win. I defended Hardy's play as the only move we could make. No one else had stepped up and John would not stop. Hardy and I knew that John was probably posturing so we weren't concerned. It was Hardy's job to fix the problem.

The next day, Hardy went to see John in his office. When he walked in, John burst out in laughter. Problem fixed.

PRE-CALL PLAN

Pre-call planning is the single most important aspect of a successful meeting. The pre-call plan is like a roadmap. Before the invention of the GPS and turn-by-turn directions, the roadmap was the traveler's most valuable tool to guide him from Point A to Point B. If there was an accident, the roadmap could redirect the driver around a traffic jam. It could also let the driver know if he or she was off track and direct them back on course. In addition, the roadmap could be used to quickly determine the driver's position on the road and estimate their arrival time.

The pre-call plan is the salesperson's roadmap. It starts with a Point A to Point B objective. For example, before calling on the data center manager, your call objective might be to "Gain commitment to move forward on the server consolidation initiative." Another call objective might be to "Get the VP of Operations to set up a meeting with the Chief Operating Officer."

When the objective is to close a sale, salespeople are usually prepared. However, I'm constantly surprised by how many salespeople I see entering a customer meeting without a call objective. The call objective should be twofold: what's in it for you and, more importantly, what's in it for the customer. Don't forget, as a CS, you must add value to your clients. If your call objective does not move you and your customer closer to accomplishing a common goal, then it is a waste of time for both of you. You have to be aware that you only get a few interactions before a customer decides that he doesn't have time to see you. That's code for "You're wasting my time because you don't bring value to our meetings."

Your clients have business meetings on a regular basis. If you are unsure why you're having a difficult time getting back in, review your meeting notes to determine exactly how you added value. Sometimes they will give you a second shot, but usually you only get one chance to demonstrate how valuable you are. [Depending on the level upon which you are calling, that number might be zero.] This means that before you are allowed to call on a C-Level executive, you should have already brought value to the managers underneath him or her.

After you have established a call objective that benefits both you and your customer, the next step is to decide how you're going to get there. The stages of a sales call vary depending on whom you ask, but here are mine:

1. Introduction and Rapport
2. Benefit Statement
3. Qualify
4. Solution Discussion
5. Trial Close
6. Objections and Questions
7. Close

Introduction and Rapport

Within each stage of the sales call, there should be a plan. What are you going to say and why is it important to the customer? If there are multiple people on the call, you should not leave decisions regarding who is going to say what up to chance. It is very awkward for a customer to see two people trying to talk over each other in a meeting. Decide in advance who will open the meeting and whether you are going to use business or personal references in the rapport phase. During the first meeting, a business reference is the safest bet. (A reference to a client's family picture on the first call may produce uncomfortable results.) When preparing, I never recommend memorizing lines because this can come across as unnatural. Rehearse the points you want to make and be prepared to key off of your customer's responses.

Benefit Statement

The initial benefit statement supports your reason for being there. "I noticed that you're spending $100 on widgets today. The industry average for these widgets is $95 and I'm here to show you how our customers are spending $90 on average." It establishes credibility by demonstrating that you know the customer's business well and have done this before.

Qualify

Many salespeople waste time with customers who are not ready to buy. They assume that, if a customer is listening to them, then they are qualified. This is often not the case because there are several reasons why customers agree to a sales meeting. Sometimes customers listen to get information in order to make a decision at a later date. Also, the person to whom you're talking could be doing research for someone else. If you are not positive that the person you're speaking with is ready, willing and able to buy from you, then you could be wasting your time. We qualify the customer by asking a simple question. "If I can show you a way to save 10% on widgets like my other customers, will you buy from me today?" The answer to this question will tell you how to proceed.

Solution Discussion

This is the meat of the call. The solution discussion should be clear and concise. If it is difficult to explain, it will be difficult to comprehend. Your facts and figures should be checked for accuracy and validated by a credible source. Missing the mark here can kill your credibility and the sale.

Trial Close

The trial close serves as an opportunity to check if you are on track with the customer. Few sales have been made during the trial close, but many have been lost. The trial close can be an assumptive statement or question: "Do you want green widgets or black?" This question will produce a response from the customer and move them into buying mode. Their response to this statement will either contain objections, indicating that the customer is not ready to buy, or reasons why they are.

Objections and Questions

I love objections because they tell you where you need to focus. The forceful objection should not be feared because they usually come from a qualified buyer. If you can satisfy these objections, you will close the sale. Questions can be objections too. If a customer asks, "Are these widgets certified?" you know the customer probably won't buy if they're not. If a customer attempts to get a better price, you must re-qualify them. For example if he or she says, "I was hoping to get a savings of 12% from you," then you have entered into a negotiation with them. In a negotiation, you never give anything away without getting confirmation in return. Your response might be, "If I can get approval to offer you a 12 percent discount, will you buy the widgets today?" If the answer is yes, then close the sale.

Close

Too many salespeople are uncomfortable with the close. You shouldn't be. If you have done your job correctly, closing the sales is a simple and logical progression that, in fact, the customer expects. In the qualifying stage, we prepared them for the close. "You said that if I can show you a way to save 10% on widgets, you would buy them from me. I'm happy to say we did it! Plus I got you an extra two percent discount. All you have to do to start receiving the savings is sign here." Get the order signed and get out. Always remember that, once you have accomplished your sales objective, it can only go downhill from there. Too many sales have been lost by a salesperson talking himself out of a closed deal. Quickly find the right moment to thank the customer and exit.

In summary, your pre-call plan is developed for each sales call based on the objective. It is the map that guides you along the road or stages of the call. Since you are prepared, you are ready to avoid potential potholes along the way. Also, if an unrelated customer issue pops up during the call, the pre-call plan will guide you back on course. At the end of the call, you can review the pre-call plan and compare it with the notes you took during the meeting. Based on your call objective, you can easily determine if the call met your objective.

As a manager, few things upset me more than the wrong answer to the question, "How did the call go?" There are two acceptable answers to this question: "It went well" or "It didn't go well." Both answers should be supported with a reason. The unacceptable answer is, "I don't know." If you haven't been observant enough throughout the process to tell whether a call has gone well or not, you haven't been doing your job. I was never an aggressive, in-your-face manager. However, I became extremely irritated with anyone that answered, "I don't know."

In our Water Institute Sales Training, I illustrate the conversation that would follow:

"So, how'd the meeting go?" I would ask.

"I don't know. Okay, I guess," the weak sales rep would say.

"You don't know? I assume you were present during the call?"

"Of course I was..."

"And I know you established a call objective that was designed to get you closer to your overall sales goal for this account," I would then interrupt.

"Eh..."

"And furthermore, I'm sure that objective was tied to your customer's business needs because our solutions are designed to solve business problems. Well, all of this would have been spelled out in your pre-call plan, anyway—mind if I take a look?" I would ask.

"I didn't do one."

"You didn't do one?" I would reply, raising my eyebrows in disbelief.

`"No, I've been trying to get in to see Ms. Customer for a while and finally got on her calendar. I wasn't sure what she would want to talk about so I went in to see."

"See what, her office?" I would grill the rep. "Let's review to make sure I understand. You are a highly trained sales representative. You've been trying to see this customer for weeks. You finally get a meeting and you walk into her office cold without understanding any of her business problems or setting an objective to meet them. And since you didn't set an objective, you didn't need a pre-call plan to guide you through your discussion.

Therefore, you're not sure how the call went. Well, I know how the call went. It went well! You set up a call with a busy executive to accomplish nothing but see her office. You met your objective!"

Once I made my point, I would soften my tone and give instruction. "What value do you think you brought to IBM or the customer?" I would ask rhetorically. Of course the answer was always "None."

"So this type of call was a waste of time," I would explain. "We only get a few opportunities to bring value to our clients. If we don't seize these moments, we might not get them again. Now before the next call you set up, I want you to review your pre-call plan with Andy. Okay?" (Andy was one of my experienced salespeople.)

I usually only had to have this conversation once. We all have our pet peeves, now you know mine. After 25 years in sales, I still do a pre-call plan for every sales meeting. Having done so many, I can usually do them in my head, though I still write down the majority of my pre-call plans.

Included in the appendix is a sample pre-call plan used in our Water Institute sales training classes.

8
THE STRATEGY

"They hate me! I can't get anyone to talk!" Hardy was beside himself.

During the deal, other parts of DialTex continued to demand his time. Win or lose, we still had to support the normal business needs of DialTex. Hardy was on his weekly pipeline call and I was pushing him on his quota shortfall when he blew up. Usually a cool cucumber, Hardy had morphed into a hot tamale. We were all feeling the stress of the DialTex deal, but Hardy was the one on the front line. Only the salesperson truly understands the difference between being insulated behind the scenes and having to deal with customer issues face-to-face. As a manager, I would try to remember what that was like before saying things like, "Just tell the customer our price increase can't be waived," or, "Tell them there's no way we can deliver before their grand opening."

Hardy's customers didn't hate him, they were just scared. I had seen this transformation many times before during outsourcing deals. Outsourcing means some clients will lose their jobs. Often your customers will try to help you if they think it might help them get hired by the outsourcer. Other times they will oppose you, thinking they can stop the deal. Walking that tightrope between using the customer to assist the deal and supporting them during these unsettling times is extremely difficult. I have found that absolute honesty is the best policy. It's another

Ralph and Sam situation. When outsourcing begins, even your closest clients know that your job is to end theirs. [Anything they tell you will be used to close the deal]. However, you owe it to them to help them find employment within your company, if at all possible.

I was uniquely qualified for these situations. Years earlier, I represented a bank client whose data center was outsourced to EDS. The rest of the client's business was managed internally. I covered the entire enterprise, which meant that both EDS and the client were my customers. During the third year of my contract, [amnesia] set in and things became tenuous. I was constantly put in a situation where I knew information that would help me close a deal at EDS but would hurt my customer. It was like the commercial where each parent says, "Don't tell Mom," and "Don't tell Dad." I was going crazy trying to keep track of what I could and couldn't say. I felt like the child in a bad marriage!

Finally, I went to each customer, sat them down and said, "We have got to do something to fix my problem! I'm struggling to keep your secrets straight. Let's set up an off-the-record policy. If there is something you need me to hold in confidence, say it's off the record. I'm trying to support you both." After that, things were marginally better but never smooth.

I wondered if this behavioral change in Hardy's customer might be a clue that they were leaning towards a GDS decision. Normally, we would position ourselves as the good guy in a bad situation. We didn't push outsourcing on the customer because, like the customer, we didn't want change. We were perfectly happy continuing our ongoing business relationship. However, when the bad guys come to take our business and our jobs, we have to respond. Our account relationships would usually produce a better flow of information for us than our competitor's. But, when this flow stopped, it could mean that the customer was planning to go with the competition. In business as in life, it's human nature to want to help those who can help you.

"You need a tissue?" I loved teasing Hardy when I got the chance because Hardy's game was very tight. He seldom got rattled. "We knew this might happen. They're scared. So poke around a little and see what's going on. But be cool."

"Poke around" meant check with security and see if you might have missed an unwanted visitor. Check with all of the C-Level assistants to see if there were any offsite meetings to Texas (GDS's headquarters). "Be cool" was all I needed to say to Hardy. He knew the drill. This was serious and he knew it.

We still had to go over Hardy's forecast though. He was trying to close a financing deal to back DialTex on $80 million of unsecured debt. They had a particularly poor credit rating. IBM Global Financing had to evaluate this opportunity [in a silo]. The outsourcing deal couldn't impact our decision. Even before the Sarbanes-Oxley Act, IBM was always concerned with obeying all accounting rules and regulations. Each employee had to certify online that they were aware of, understood and agreed to follow all IBM Business Conduct Guidelines. Any display of favoritism during this deal could bring unwanted attention from the Feds. But not backing the $80 million would create a less favorable selling environment. IBM Global Financing agreed to finance DialTex if they secured it with an Irrevocable Letter of Credit. In other words, we said no, because, if they had this letter of credit, they probably wouldn't need IBM to back them. Essentially, they had asked us for a favor and we had turned them down.

Hardy and I discussed the rest of his shortfall and developed his gap plan to make it up. We had to go through this futile pipeline exercise because our jobs required us to play our roles. But we knew Hardy would either hit a grand slam this year or be sent down to the minors. The difference between winning and losing was that great for him.

That evening, Hardy called my mobile phone. "Hathaway was in there. They signed him in under another name. Sneaky suckers." Kemper Hathaway was GDS's World Wide EVP of Sales. He was the heir apparent to the CEO and was world-renowned for ruthlessly closing deals at any cost. "He met with Robert Hill one-on-one behind closed doors for about an hour. He and his team left smiling," Hardy reported.

"Son of a gun!" I said, restraining myself. Hill was DialTex's CEO! We knew this decision was going to be made by the COO, Tony Gaudenza, and we had him covered. However, it didn't look good for the competition to call on the CEO when we hadn't. We had no way of knowing if Hill was going to influence this decision, or if something else had changed.

"Okay, we've got to develop an executive call strategy," I said. An executive call strategy is basically a "We can, too" exercise to ensure that the customer's most senior executives feel like we know and care about them and their business. Although our CEO, Dick Tomlinson, and our VP of Sales, Jerry Dork, had called on Gaudenza, Hathaway's visit changed things. Because Hathaway was calling on DialTex so late in the deal, it meant he was trying to offer something big to close them as soon as possible.

"You think he backed the $80 million?" I asked, knowing we had to put our executives in front of Hill immediately. It had to be someone who had the authority to make major decisions on the spot.

"Heck yeah!" Hardy exclaimed. "Either straight up or as part of the deal. We gotta get Dick back in there quick."

I had a different idea. "If Gaudenza is going to throw it in our face, I don't want that situation to blow up on us. Besides, we can't get Dick that quickly, so Dork is our only option from the sales side. Let's get Braxton in there."

Bob Braxton was IBM Global Services SVP of North America. He also happened to be an old college buddy of mine. Although I would never admit it to Bob, I considered him to be one of the few salespeople at IBM whose game was better than mine. Bob did everything well. He was in high demand and hard to get.

"Can we get him?" Hardy asked.

"I'll get him," I assured.

"Oh, yeah," Hardy said, recalling our relationship.

I continued to explain my strategy. "Bob will definitely cover Gaudenza, but we'll need to find a way to also get him in front of Hill [before Dick calls on him]."

"Dork is going to be *pissed!*" Hardy laughed. Everyone knew Braxton and Dork were both pushing for the North America General Manager job. Whoever closed this deal would have a leg up.

"I know, that's why it's going to be your idea," I laughed. "Look, you set up the meeting with Bob Braxton and Gaudenza first. But make sure Hill is also available on the same day. Call his assistant to schedule a five-minute pop-in with Hill on the way to the Gaudenza meeting. Call me as soon as possible when you get them." I paused to give Hardy time to work out the arrangements in his head.

"Meanwhile, I'll contact Dork's office to schedule him and Hill for a one-on-one on the same day," I explained. "I'll get him juiced up to go in for the close. We'll blame the scheduling mix-up on you forgetting to tell me about Bob and I'll cover you."

"Okay, but what if Bob calls Dork fir..?" Hardy stopped himself, once again remembering our relationship. It is standard protocol for IBM executives at Bob and Dork's level to have a briefing document and communicate with each other prior to making a call like this. But Bob would understand the situation and do me the favor.

"I got Bob. You get things set up at DialTex." The executive call strategy was set.

The meetings were set for the following Wednesday and I briefed Dork, explaining that Hardy was "busy." It seemed as though we were going to be able to pull it off until the morning of the call when Dork called Hardy for a last minute update. Hardy told him everything—except that Bob was there.

He hung up with Dork and called me saying, "I'm in trouble!" He explained the situation.

"Look, you made the right move. We've gotta play this thing out as planned. We can't risk Dork screwing up this deal. Now don't worry, stay focused and execute the plan. I've got your back." I hung up the phone and said to myself, *Hardy's in trouble.*

The calls went masterfully well. Bob did what he always does and got Gaudenza back in our camp. Bob found out that GDS was cheaper and more flexible than us. Flexibility means concessions. Contractually, IBM was often less flexible than our competition. Our contracts were not changed a great deal. We had to rely more on faith and a handshake. Because our business relationships touched the customer in so many different ways, [our flexibility was often a change in a separate and unrelated revenue stream and not in the contract at hand]. Bob left Hill primed and ready and then met with Gaudenza. He convinced them to allow us to recommend additional changes to DialTex's existing hardware platform. This was not allowed in the original customer requirements. The more IBM products we could include in the contract, the more flexibility we would have. Obviously, Bob couldn't speak knowledgeably regarding the configurations, so he bought us two weeks to augment our proposal.

Dork's call also went very well with Hill. We left knowing that DialTex preferred IBM to GDS if we could work out the big price difference. However, Dork did find out about Bob Braxton. We knew this was going to happen so I had planned to call Bob when he was on his way to DialTex. Now I was kicking myself for having missed that detail with Bob. I knew he had to call Dork out of respect, but I forgot to tell him that I wanted to call Dork first. By the time Hardy called me, it was too late. Dork was livid when he got me on the phone.

"What in heck kinda territory are you running? How could you guys forget to call me on this?!" he shouted.

"Look, Jerry, Hardy forgot to tell me. He's been under a lot of pressure with DialTex and Jakumi." I tried to diffuse his outrage. Jakumi was Hardy's other account and was a very large Internet service provider at that time. "He had Jakumi at the briefing center and saw Bob. They talked about DialTex and set up the call. I just found out." Dork was no dummy, he knew Bob and me too well. He also knew Bob would corroborate my story so there was nothing he could do to me.

"Okay, but why in the world didn't Hardy tell me? We talked five minutes before the call. I want him off the account!" The line went dead.

Dork was just trying to apply pressure. He was mad and had the power to make Hardy's life difficult, but he couldn't just pull him in the middle of a billion-dollar deal. I would have to let things cool off and deal with Dork later. Hardy would never know how close things came to disaster. As his manager, I promised to cover him, and I did.

WHAT YOU DON'T KNOW CAN HURT YOU

Knowledge wins most deals. We need to be in the "I know" business, not the "I think" business. In any deal, we have to know the answers to the following basic questions:

- What does the customer want?
- Who do they perceive has the best solution?
- Is there any buzz on the competitor's offering?
- Who is in the know? (Who is our customer contact?)
- Has anything changed in the approval process or criteria?
- Who are our inside sales people? (Who are our customer sponsors?)

During the DialTex deal, we answered all of these questions in the beginning but, as we entered the Build the Solution phase, we continued to validate and adjust our assumptions. In the beginning, the entire solution depends on the answer to the first question. But things change when a customer talks to different vendors about the same business problem. They start to hear vendor's various approaches to solving these issues and, as a result, will change what they want.

This information will start to permeate the organization, and the successful CS must constantly ask questions and look for clues that something has changed. These changes will invariably come out in meetings, even if they are unrelated to the deal. There are many moving parts that require validation during large services deals. For example, if your competitor's data back-up strategy is suddenly perceived as more efficient than yours, you might start getting questions about your strategy. To uncover potential shifts like these, I would ask the same questions repeatedly of multiple people throughout the account. I generally disguise the questions so the customer doesn't think I'm fishing, but I make sure to get the important questions answered several times by numerous people. Law enforcement uses this technique regularly and the objective is to provide the interrogator more opportunities to catch a slip-up or alteration in someone's story. Often a person *wants* to tell you something and just needs the right environment to do so. If you have a strong relationship with the customer, this information will usually come out right away. If the customer wants you to win, he will often tell you where your solution is weak so that you can fix it.

As we went through the questioning process at DialTex, I was reminded of the worst loss of my career. I had a very good customer who only bought IBM mainframes. During early discussions to upgrade the customer's install base, one of my inside reps said, "You know, HDS is claiming that their mainframes are faster."

That one comment told me that the deal had changed. This was no longer going to be our usual price negotiation. This was now a competitive situation in which HDS had visited my customer and pitched their new box. I needed to do my homework on HDS's mainframe to see if their claims were true. I knew that processor speed was second only to reliability in importance to this customer because they processed very large volumes of complex financial data that was extremely time-sensitive. Every second faster could mean millions in savings.

It would be disastrous if HDS was faster than IBM. At that time, mainframes were everything to IBM. Not only did they represent hundreds of millions of dollars of hardware revenue, they also brought in software and maintenance revenue streams. Furthermore, the prestige of owning the datacenter was undeniably important. It meant that you controlled the account and could leverage against the mainframe on just about everything else you did.

It turned out that their claim was substantiated. Soon every trade and business magazine, in addition to most newspapers (including the *Wall Street Journal*), had a feature story about our mainframe's demise. Because of the comment that surfaced during questioning, I knew the competitor's strategy. We did everything possible to test and benchmark the customer's workloads to fight HDS, but ultimately, we couldn't beat them. We lost the deal. But being in the know at least gave us a fighting chance.

Losing a mainframe deal as the incumbent, we not only lost the current deal, but all our machines and the associated revenue streams would be displaced as well. I was devastated because this was an account that I had built from nothing to a $15 million per year customer. It was the worst loss of my career. In fact, it was the only year in my career that I missed the 100 percent Sales Club. Even my customers felt awful for me and took me to a local pub to drown my sorrows!

The beauty of information technology is that it is a leapfrog industry. A company might have an absolute competitive advantage one month and find itself ranked third a few months later. IBM was beaten by HDS because we were changing our mainframe technology. When the new processor was introduced, it was smaller, cooler and faster—faster than HDS. As soon as the new machines were announced, I attacked with a vengeance to win back the mainframe.

There was plenty of buzz in the press so I capitalized on it. "How would you like to be one of the first customers in the world to have our new mainframe? I mean before GE, GM or JP Morgan." I knew this level of prestige would mean a great deal to them. "We'll have to start now, I'll arrange a briefing at our Poughkeepsie plant."

The next month, we rented transportation and took ten IT managers to New York so that our smartest techies could wow my customer with IBM's plans to rule the mainframe platform forever. I realize that this sounds far-fetched, but that is exactly what IBM did. Today, IBM has almost no competition in the mainframe space. Its two largest competitors, Amdahl and HDS, are no longer threats. At the time, without proof, our claims were a difficult proposition for customers to swallow.

Before my customer arrived, I visited the plant to ensure that everything was going to run smoothly. This is something that I always did whenever possible. I met the briefing coordinator and all of the speakers. We discussed my client's needs and my strategy for a successful briefing. I also talked to the system engineers who were analyzing the customer's data.

The lead engineer was an absolute Einstein whose name, quite appropriately, was Guru. My customers got a real kick out that coincidence! We were confident that we were faster, but I needed to be sure and I wanted to know *how much* faster. I grilled Guru.

"How much faster are we than HDS?" I got right to the point. If he could confidently tell me we were 10 to 15 percent faster, I could breathe easier.

"Twenty percent," Guru said.

My breathing and shoulders immediately relaxed.

We'd won. All we had to do now was watch the deal play out like a movie. We were now so assured of victory that we each placed bets as to *exactly* how fast we thought the new mainframe would be. I won!

Now that the business stage was set, I could plan the entertainment. I visited the best steakhouse in town, made reservations, picked our table, discussed a Service Level Agreement and tipped the manager 50 percent in advance. I got tickets to the Knicks basketball game and arranged to have limousines take us to Madison Square Garden. I instructed the drivers to listen to the game on the radio and be ready to pick us up at the curb as soon as the game was over. It's important to know how to plan a successful customer meeting or trip, including entertainment. Even if the events are not extravagant, thoughtful details tailored to a customer's preferences always go a long way.

KNOW THE APPROVAL PROCESS

It's critical to know the approval process for your accounts. In most organizations, procedures change during the decision-making or approval process regularly. Many factors such as new management, budget constraints and federal regulations can change or delay the process of closing a deal. You cannot assume that you know how to get a new deal closed because you have closed a similar one in that account before. In addition, you cannot assume that your customer knows the process just because he thinks he does. I once saw an IT manager fired for this assumption.

Bill was my client and we were working on a check processing solution. The technology had just changed to allow the magnetic ink character recognition (MICR) to be read by our check sorter and an electronic image to be captured. This new technology was superior and a no-brainer when compared to our previous sorting machines. Together, we did the cost justification analysis and the deal looked great. Bill had approval authority (or so he thought) because it fell within his dollar threshold. I had done deals with him before, so I didn't validate his authority. He signed, placed the order and we patted each other on the back for a job well done. I would look good for selling one of our new machines, and Bill would look good for introducing a new cost-saving technology to his company. What we didn't know was that IBM was already working with Bill's headquarters on a large deal to replace all of their locations' machines with this new technology. Neither of us were aware of this project.

When Bill's CIO found out, he was not happy with his reckless behavior because it wasn't the first time Bill had pulled this stunt. Bill wanted to make a name for himself as a leader and often acted before he received permission. This time, he knew he'd pushed it too far and, when I ran into him at a restaurant a few weeks later, he asked me if I knew of any job opportunities with my other clients. It was a hard way to learn this lesson which might have been avoided had I taken the time to learn who the real decision-maker was.

Knowing who the influencers and decision-makers are is especially important in an outsourcing deal. In my current sales consulting engagements at Marketing and Business Integration, we see more mistakes in this area than any other. Many salespeople assume that, if they have closed a deal with VP-level approval in the past, this VP can also approve a services outsourcing deal at the same or lesser dollar amount. This is usually not true.

Remember how I discussed the fact that DialTex would have all of their eggs in IBM's basket if we won the deal? Well, the same would go for any outsourcing deal. Outsourcing purchases are not analyzed the same way by every organization. Of course the cost-benefit analysis is evaluated, but the vendor risk is of utmost importance. In other words, your customer won't care how much they're saving if you're breaking their eggs. Outsourcing can be a fundamental change in how the organization runs its business. Therefore, most outsourcing deals endure a much greater degree of scrutiny by senior management than their routine purchase counterparts.

KNOW HOW TO FIGHT CLIENT AMNESIA

It's important to briefly talk about the evolution of multi-term deals from the opposing views of the customer and the provider. Companies don't generally ask an outside vendor to come into their organization and run a slice of their business when things are going well. There is usually a significant business problem that requires a solution. In the beginning, the customer will often come to you desperate, openly describing the pain of their business problems. Even if they are not open, the provider will quickly uncover these problems as they analyze the current business processes.

By the time year three of the contract concludes, however, customers develop an acute case of amnesia. They have no memory of how bad things were when you first showed up. This is partly because they believe it and partly because they're posturing. Once they have given you their basket, any broken eggs become your problem. They are paying you a large sum of money to fix the existing cracks and not cause any new ones, and the pressure on your customer to beat their competition doesn't subside just because you are involved. In fact, it becomes quite easy for them to blame the outsourcing contract when other parts of their business are sputtering. You become an easy target. The question arises, "Whose idea was this anyway?" And no one ever seems to remember.

This amnesia is a serious disease. It can quickly spread throughout the organization until one day you show up and your customer asks, "What are you doing here? You guys were fired yesterday." It's a tough illness to cure, so prevention is the best remedy.

To prevent amnesia, give your customer a regular CAP (Customer Appreciation Program) Pill. The purpose of the CAP Pill or CAP letter is threefold:

- To demonstrate a display of appreciation for your customer's business.
- To reinforce the baseline for the contract's Service Level Agreement (SLA).
- To recognize the solutions to business problems you and the customer have developed jointly.

The frequency of the dosage will depend upon your business needs. Many contracts require monthly or at least quarterly reviews to assess performance, review the Service Level Agreement and establish new agreements for additional requirements added during the contract. At a minimum, every customer should receive a CAP letter annually whether it is an outsourced contract or not.

Selling and supporting service contracts is more difficult than product contracts mainly due to the human aspect of the offering. For example, hardware is plugged in, programmed and then run. Services engagements require the customer's personnel to work with the provider's personnel. Customers are required to make more emotional decisions so the CS needs to be heavily involved throughout the entire Consultative Sales Cycle to ensure that the sales and ongoing support run smoothly.

9
THE DISASTER AND DISTRACTIONS

It had been three weeks since orals. The customer was leaning our way but we were still in a serious competitive battle. The pressure continued to build as time went on. Unlike an official request for proposal process where there are strict rules and stringent deadlines, the DialTex deal was a fluid process. Things were constantly changing. DialTex was working to get the best deal it could for its business. The only firm date was December 31st because they wanted this deal to be closed and announced by the end of their fiscal year. Given the financial, legal and technical work that was required between acceptance and contract signature, we had about a month before DialTex needed to make a decision.

By September, I was happy that the DialTex deal was in a lull. One of the large consulting firms had sold IBM another multi-million dollar reengineering and restructuring plan for its sales process. We were not immune to spending too much for things we did not necessarily need. Once purchased, our executives had to justify the existence of their new toys so the management teams were commissioned to implement and enforce the new plan as if we had designed it ourselves. I found it extremely hard to convincingly sell the new directives to my team as if I supported them. Over my career, I had moved from drinking the corporate Kool-Aid, to gulping it in several flavors, to now, preferring tea. In the past, I prided myself on my ability to enthusiastically promote and implement some of the most absurd changes with my team. They always believed that I liked the idea because I could cite multiple reasons why it would be good for our business. But, by this point, a few of my employees had called me out on some of my statements because they could clearly see through my act.

I began to realize that IBM was changing faster than I was and we were growing apart. I challenged authority more and even the most routine activities were beginning to tax me. I was burning out. I had voiced this to my manager some time earlier and we had devised a plan to find something within IBM that I would find new and exciting. After all, at IBM, you can change careers or continents and still keep the same ID badge. In order to determine if a higher level on the same career path would suit me, I was assigned to fill in for my manager while he was away. When he returned, I told him that the only job I hated more than mine was his! That didn't go over very well. I didn't see anywhere to go but out, and I began to accept that, whether we won or lost this deal, I was probably going to leave IBM.

I prepared for the two-day meeting with my cluster. (That's right, I was not running a branch or a business unit, I was now running a cluster. I have never been able to bring myself to understand how our leaders accepted this change in nomenclature. I couldn't find one colleague or customer who thought this presented IBM in a more favorable way to our clients.)

I wanted to help the members of my team have a leadership role. This was partly for their career development and partly because I didn't feel like doing the work. Some of the process was validating. We were asked to take our teams through a historical review of the old days when IBM flooded our accounts with resources and was viewed as the darling of the industry. As I discussed the old organizational structure and processes, I longed for the good old days. I understood that many of these changes were out of necessity—we simply couldn't be profitable the old way. Our competitors were smarter and more nimble than before. It was ironic how the products we sold were being used against us! Technology was allowing very small companies to be very big players. However, I still disagreed with many of our changes and realized that, in fact, I wasn't leaving IBM, IBM had left me a long time ago. It wasn't the company's fault entirely. Corporate America had changed as a whole.

At 8:30 on the morning of September 11th, I was going over the agenda with Andy, one of my sales managers. As we reviewed his slides in preparation for the cluster meeting, my assistant, Barb, knocked on the door and poked her head in.

"I just heard that a small commuter plane crashed into the World Trade Center," she said.

"Wow," I replied. "Poor guy. I hope no one else was hurt."

Andy and I continued with our preparations until Barb appeared in the doorway again, shaken.

"It was actually a passenger jet," she reported.

This was different. The potential loss of life was far greater. I asked Barb to roll in my TV and the three of us watched the awful scene unfold until the second plane hit. At that moment, we knew that America was under attack.

"I'm going home," Andy said abruptly, gathering his files.

Time stopped. The cluster meeting preparation stopped. The DialTex deal stopped. All I could think about was my family and the poor people tragically killed. I called my wife and told her to leave work and go home. I went to get the kids from daycare. I got everyone safely home and turned on the TV. When the two towers collapsed, I was speechless. I had colleagues in New York! IBM didn't have a standard procedure for this, but we knew we had to account for all of our people.

I started making phone calls to my team. All but one were accounted for by about 2:00 p.m. The person missing was a sales rep in Washington, D.C., whose father worked at the Pentagon in the impact zone where American Airlines Flight 77 crashed. I was hopeful that the only reason we couldn't reach him was because he was busy trying to locate his dad in the midst of the chaos. (We would learn the next day that, fortunately, his father was in a meeting on the other side of the building and not harmed.)

My other peers who ran territories in New York were not as fortunate. They had to deal with friends, family and colleagues affected by the tragedy. My friend, Ray Brown, the track star, was working for a large New York City investment firm located in a building adjacent to the Twin Towers. When I called to check on him the next day, he described his horrific experience.

Ray was stunned when he looked out his window and saw people jumping from the Towers to their deaths. He left his office when the South Tower collapsed and ran in panic until he was able to duck into a store to try to escape the suffocating dust cloud that had invaded the streets. Others climbed over each other, choking, trying to take cover from the cloud. Eventually, Ray made it home safely.

He was one of the lucky ones.

The next day was supposed to be the cluster meeting, but we postponed it for a week instead. Many of us were back in the office, but no one was working. We spent the entire day comforting and talking to each other. When I talked to Hardy, the only mention of the DialTex deal was that he would let me know if they contacted him for help.

So many of our customers needed help. Many found parts of their operations crippled because of the attacks. Several companies, including IBM, had sold disaster recovery solutions designed to provide customers with computers, network communications and a facility to run their businesses when a disaster is declared. Customers had monthly contracts that clearly specified the parameters of their backup solution. Periodically, their disaster recovery plans were tested and the customer ran their business in the provider's data center.

Before 9/11, this was a profitable and valuable business for IBM and other service providers. Customers liked it because they had a plausible disaster recovery plan that they could present to their clients and their boards. September 11th changed all of that. These contracts were never designed to protect customers from a catastrophic regional disaster. If a customer had a fire or water damage in their data center, their disaster recovery plan would back them up well. However, none of these providers had the facilities to support their customers if they all declared disasters at once.

Many providers offered a first-come-first-served policy. Once they were full, everyone else had to wait. On 9/11, dozens of customers were literally left outside the building when they declared disasters to their service providers. These companies suffered tremendous financial losses and several went out of business. All of our customers and many of our competitors came to IBM for help and we were lauded for our efforts to support them. It wasn't smooth and not everyone was happy, but at the end of the day, I was proud of how IBM performed during this crisis.

The disaster recovery industry changed as a result of the tragedy. Before 9/11, most disaster recovery plans were a joke—insufficient plans on paper meant to appease auditors and regulators. After the tragedy, they transformed from something businesses could perfunctorily check off their list into a fire, bomb, flood and earthquake proof failsafe that would allow business to run even if Mars attacked. Large companies moved to an internal model and built backup data centers in other regions. Smaller companies secured dedicated space from disaster recovery providers that was often isolated and fenced off from the company's provider. At Marketing and Business Integration, my current company, I've provided access to several of these sites and they are all very impressive. I have one client who can, at a moment's notice, run the entire business from one of its five data centers around the world.

We spent the rest of that tragic week ensuring that our customers had all of the support we could give them. In the back of my mind, I knew that disaster recovery efforts would impact our deal at DialTex for the better.

I'm often amazed at the resilience of mankind. The way we rebound and rebuild after an earthquake or major hurricane is phenomenal. Life goes on. This was never more evident than after 9/11. The way I felt after that horrible Tuesday, how could I get up and sell this cluster change to my team just six days later?

I started the meeting asking everyone to share their experiences from 9/11. Some openly spoke in detail and others didn't want to say anything. It was cathartic and allowed us to move on to business.

I began with a detailed history of the good old days when I started with IBM. The process was designed to pull things from the past and incorporate them into our future plan. As I described the history of our 12- to 18-month training program, our client coverage model and old branch meetings, I recalled all of the people who had moved on and I missed the old days. [I also realized that IBM had changed to such an extent that our change in nomenclature might as well have started with our name. We were that different.]

More administrative work and fewer support resources equaled less customer face time for sales reps. One internal survey revealed that most salespeople were spending more than half of their time involved with activities in the office, away from the customer. While the change may have been necessary, it was hard for me to swallow. Knowing I'd be moving on made winning DialTex an even bigger prize. I wanted to go out on a win.

As I transitioned to presenting the specifics of the new plan, I noticed Hardy was less attentive than usual. He never paid close attention to this kind of stuff, but I had to give him and Andy the eye a couple of times. Finally, he got up and walked out of the meeting. *Perhaps he's distracted by the events of the week,* I thought. *I hope it's a problem with DialTex and not something personal.* The attack had really put things in perspective for me. The deal that had engulfed our lives for nearly nine months paled in comparison to the previous week's challenges. I could handle a business problem—that's what I did, and did well.

I called a recess and went to find Hardy.

"What the heck was that about in there?" I asked.

"Sorry. It was DialTex. We needed to discuss our disaster recovery plan. Understandably, everyone's disaster recovery plan now has to be presented in detail and approved by their board."

"We already have our plan in the proposal," I said.

"Yeah, but we have to go through another Q&A focused on just the plan."

"Okay, this isn't bad. We can show better than GDS here," I reassured.

I didn't like what I was thinking. During my IBM career, I have seen reps capitalize on a customer's misfortunes a few times. When a data center floods or catches on fire, it has to be replaced. These bluebirds of opportunity could instantly make a rep's quota. Of course, no one wished misfortune on his customer and we felt sorry about the impact on their business. But you wouldn't be able to tell this by the office celebration after a bluebird flew in and landed on the lucky rep's desk. I knew one rep that actually had two of his customers' data centers flood a few years apart. He once joked, "My year looks bleak, might have to call Vito again."

But this was different. I couldn't feel good about profiting from 9/11 in any way. We were already hearing about the scare tactics being used by some disaster recovery companies to entice customers into buying their services. We were not like them. However, regardless of how it came about, disaster recovery was now a bona fide customer need. If our services were better, we needed to let them know. This was really no different than the 99.999 percent availability and reliability standards we touted for mainframes every day.

"Are you busy?" Hardy asked. I had zoned out as he was talking.

"Yeah, good, get IBM Global Services to craft the response and schedule the meeting ASAP."

Hardy again stared at me, waiting for a response. "Yes, you can leave, come by and sign the certification later," I said. (All employees had to certify that they were present, had heard and understood our new cluster changes. Hardy was happy to escape the remainder of the six-hour ordeal.)

"Later!" he declared, leaving before I changed my mind and he lost the sale.

Yet another distraction came a few days later, when I was asked to hear an IBM personnel case. IBM had an open door policy where an employee could freely escalate a grievance if he or she felt they were being treated unfairly. When a situation was sensitive, a manager from another location could be called to assist. This was designed to demonstrate objectivity because the outside manager was only selected if he or she knew nothing about the case.

"Scott, you have got to be kidding me! Right now?" I argued. "I mean, it's not like I'm busy trying to make my third quarter numbers or implement this masterful cluster reorganization. Oh, and did I miss DialTex closing this morning? If not, I might need to focus on that deal as well!"

Scott went on to explain, "Green asked me for this personally. This one is visible and sensitive. You're the closest one to that location who I trust. You can get in and out in a day. I'll make sure James knows what a swell guy you are." That was code for "you'll get good exposure on this case." James Green was our VP of Human Resources and reported directly to Dick Tomlinson, our CEO. He was a good person to owe you one.

"Fine, the People's Court calls and I get to go play Judge Freakin' Wapner for a day. I'll go get my black robe dry-cleaned," I retorted.

I was actually seeing the benefit of this opportunity, but I couldn't give in without getting something in return. "How are the Master's tickets coming?" I asked. IBM spared no expense when it came to sponsoring or treating our customers to a great experience at the premier PGA golf event each year. These were some of the hardest tickets to get in the company—or for any golf fan for that matter.

Scott laughed. "I'm working on them."

The case was an absolute mess. It could have been a human resources case study. The employee was being fired for poor performance. His manager was in a romantic relationship with the second line manager. The terminated employee accused both managers of racism and conspiring against him. The witnesses were split, but didn't like any parties involved. The employee's manager had another employee who had a grievance regarding an unrelated incident with an old boyfriend. All involved in this soap opera were right out of college and had been at IBM for less than four years. I used to think the sales offices were full of drama, but it was clear that manufacturing had us beat.

So much for "in and out in a day." It took two full days to hear, rule and write the summary that read like an episode of "The Jerry Springer Show". I was beginning to think that our hiring standards had slipped a bit, and I had to run three miles each day to keep my head from exploding. On top of the DialTex deal and other business distractions, this was the last thing I needed to spend my time doing.

When I got back to the office, I got a call from Julia, one of my junior sales reps. She was preparing for her first solo C-Level call to the CFO of a small utility company. Julia was nervous and needed some reassurance. Her account and pre-call plans were sound so I focused on strategy. I reviewed with her my approach for calling on C-Level executives. Although quite experienced with executive sales calls, Hardy and I would need these strategy reminders later in our own deal.

THE C-LEVEL CALL

In our training classes, one of the things we stress when calling on the C-Level is that there is no cookie cutter approach. So much that is written about this topic seems to oversimplify it. Some companies develop a C-Level sales pitch, but this is the wrong approach. It's similar to the car salesman that thought he knew the car I wanted as soon as I walked in the door. The information that you present to the C-Level has to be valuable to their organization and that information varies from company to company. You have to earn the right to advise any customer about their business. Most of our training centers around calling on the CIO and CFO, but our approach is relevant for any C-Level call. Since, in many organizations, the CIO frequently reports to the CEO, I devised the 5-P approach to work in preparation for any C-Level call.

THE 5 - P APPROACH

Person

Over the last several years, the role of the CIO has changed dramatically. CIO's are now business people who spend more time solving business problems and less time improving IT operations. In fact, in *CIO Magazine*'s 2010 State of the CIO Survey, almost 90% of the CIO's polled expected to have an additional leadership roll outside of IT within three to five years. They planned to spend more than 50% of their time driving innovation and less than 10% negotiating with IT vendors. Try pushing a canned C-Level sales pitch on one of these guys and you'll be guaranteed failure.

If the role is changing, so are the people seeking out that role. You need to do your research. What have they published? What is their leadership style? Are they a star within the company? What do they like? They might prefer a chalk-talk to a PowerPoint presentation. The Internet makes this type of information so readily available that there is no excuse for not knowing.

Finally, talk to his or her managers and assistants. They will tell you a great deal about the CIO's hot buttons, dislikes and expectations.

Purpose

The first thing you need to decide is when is the best time to contact the C-Level executive. What is the purpose of getting in front of them? Do you need this person involved to accomplish your objective, or are you just calling high because you were told to do so? You cannot waste touches at this level because you only get a few. The purpose of your call needs to not only add value to the customer but also move you closer to solving an overall objective. I have been very successful selling to companies with little or no C-Level involvement, so it is not always necessary. You must first ensure that you need the C-Level executive before you call.

According to the 2010 Survey, more than 35% of CIO's polled delegate more responsibility to trusted lieutenants in order to elevate their position within the company. Other companies continue to have the CIO integrally involved in all major IT decisions. My rule is, if I don't need the CIO or if I can't add value, I won't waste their time or mine with a useless meeting. Also, don't bore them with needless, probing questions about their initiatives that should have been answered by their managers beforehand. I have cancelled or postponed C-Level meetings because my team was ill-prepared.

Additionally, the discussion should be centered on the value you bring to the customer's business, not your products. You're the only one in the meeting that cares about your products. The C-Level only cares about viable solutions to their business problems. If you're a salesperson who prides yourself on speeds-and-feeds discussions, you may be a very good product specialist, but you shouldn't be the one calling on the C-Level executive. At IBM, I could bring in 1,000 people who knew our products better than me, but I could never find anyone who knew my customer better.

People

In most cases, you have been working with their management team before you have an opportunity to call on the C-Level. Use this time wisely and remember that their initiatives come from above. By the time you get to the C-Level, you should be prepared to discuss these pressing initiatives. You earned the right to call at the C-Level because of your strong relationships below. The C-Level meeting should be a validation of everything you have accomplished with their team. The discussion should be centered around how your solution can help their business initiatives, not determining what they are. I have even used this approach in the few cases where the CIO call had to be the first call. If none of his managers would talk, I would seek out his assistant, a consistently valuable and informative resource who wants the CIO's meetings to be productive as well.

Proof

In sales we are constantly trying to prove ourselves to clients. This proof is called "establishing credibility". In our training classes, we frequently remind our students that credibility is the number one asset a CS possesses.

Demonstrating a solid knowledge of your client's business needs and how to meet them is only a start. Even when your ideas are accepted at this level, you still have to prove that you (and your company) can deliver. This is where the Initial Benefit Statement comes in. "John Doe at XYZ Company had a similar requirement and I saved them 15 percent." We've found that this "Been There, Done That" sales technique is very powerful.

Since almost 70% of today's CIO's report to the CFO or CEO, you need to assume that you are selling to all three simultaneously. As discussed in Chapter 1, the cost-benefit analysis is an important step as you build the business case. This is how the C-Level makes investment decisions. They look at the Return on Investment (ROI), not the price. Remember, ROI is a *value* discussion not a *price* discussion. Price discussions are reserved for product specialists and purchasing managers, not the C-Level and the CS.

Finally, leave the C-Level executive with a deal sheet summarizing the important aspects of the solution. Make sure you highlight the opportunity cost on the deal sheet. This is the cost they'll incur for not doing business with you. The savings or benefit can't start until the customer acts. Then, get out. Remember, their time is limited. Save some for a later visit.

Politics

Understanding the politics of a customer is very

important and takes time. You can't assume you have a new friend because you've met with the C-Level executive. They rarely find us as interesting as we find ourselves, therefore, we have to use brevity in all of our correspondence. They don't have time to read a three-page e-mail. Keep e-mails to a few sentences, but make those sentences count. I frequently spend 15-20 minutes crafting a five-sentence e-mail to ensure that I get my point across succinctly without stepping on anyone's toes in the organization. I know the executive (and his assistant) usually only reads about five sentences anyway so the challenge is to get all of my points across in that space. Whatever you do, don't flood them with voice messages and e-mails. They will respond to substance, not volume. And they will often respond through an assistant or subordinate, so measure your effectiveness by assessing *if* you received a response rather than *who* responded.

Finally, you have to ensure that you are not upsetting your client by dealing directly with the C-Level too frequently. C-Level access is very important, but so are your relationships below. Some clients get nervous when salespeople regularly call on the C-Level because they're afraid of being excluded from influencing decisions that affect them. Therefore, your instincts will have to guide you to strike the perfect balance of dealing with both levels.

10
THE CLOSE

In the final weeks before DialTex made a decision, we were
on site everyday fulfilling our ongoing sales and support
duties. However, there was little we could do to advance
the Billion-Dollar Deal. DialTex went dark—no one was
giving us anything. Our careers hung on this deal and
there was nothing more I could do to control it. We were
now in the toughest stage of the Consultative Sales Cycle:
The Wait.

Adding to the tension, our "help"—those vultures
circling to take credit for our win or rejoice at our failure—
had us locked in an internal political battle. I constantly
had to defend our sales efforts, customer relationships
and sales team against all of the internal second-guessing
that had grown from a murmur to an outright roar. This
"help" was spreading the word that we might lose the deal.
Of course they would say, "We did everything possible to
overcome the deficiencies of the sales team, but their
weaknesses were too great." They walked a tightrope,
struggling to stay close enough to take credit for a win, yet
remain a safe distance away from the blame of a loss. In 25
years of sales, I've never had anyone come into one of my
accounts and say, "Sorry, I really messed up this deal for
you guys, I'll be sure to let everyone know it was my fault."
In corporate sales, this came with the territory. That said,
I couldn't go to any meeting in the region without

someone asking if there was anything they could do to "help."

Then things got worse. I was in my office and Barb buzzed me. "Dick's office is on the line." Taking the call, I learned that Dick Tomlinson, our CEO, wanted to call on Tony Gaudenza, DialTex's COO, to see if he could *save* the deal. Save was a carefully chosen political word—the deal didn't need saving. Framing his visit this way would put Dick in a no-lose situation.

My team went through the fire drill again, preparing and setting up the call. Since Dick and Tony were former rivals when Tony was at IBM, there was the risk that the meeting could blow up on us. As hard as Dick was to get any other time, I thought it was strange that he would show up twice on our deal. It was big, but it wasn't the only large deal happening at IBM.

I called Hardy to offer a calming hand. "Dick wants another meeting with Tony so I need you to be okay with it."

"I am," he said. "It might actually be a good idea."

"You remember their first call wasn't exactly a hit?" I pushed him because, in this situation, I knew that a passive Hardy was worse than an angry Hardy. I was concerned that he was becoming desperate, anticipating a loss. I trusted his instincts, so if he was scared, then I was too.

"No, but things are too quiet," he reasoned. "He's not going to do anything to help, but he might shake things up enough to open a dialogue for me."

"Okay, set it up but don't make it look easy." Hardy was right. He would have to talk to multiple people at DialTex to schedule the meeting. He was savvy enough to get some type of read on the situation from that number of client interactions. "Don't make it look easy" meant to let everyone know that Dick was coming and that the account team would take the lead to find a way to get this meeting scheduled without an issue. He would schedule a big preparation conference call to assign action items and responsibility to the IBM Global Services team. In other words, "Don't let them take us for granted."

"Call me later, I want to run something by you," I said.

I was working on an idea. Wouldn't it be great if there was some negative press about GDS floating around? Even with the recent events, this deal appeared to be coming down to a price decision. IBM didn't usually win on price. We were the safe decision, the partner who provided added value. You might pay a little more, but we were worth it. A little negative press about GDS could help tilt the scales just enough our way.

I asked the team for help during our next pipeline call. [The pipeline call was a weekly cadence when I reviewed important deals with the team. Each one of my client managers and sales reps would take me through his or her forecast and discuss situations where they needed help. At the end, I would ask for their "take it to the bank" numbers that I would roll up to my manager.] I usually scheduled these calls in half-hour intervals, but periodically I would have one big call so that the entire team could hear. Communication and knowledge transfer is often difficult in large companies. This provided the team with an opportunity to hear something that might help them close one of their deals.

But, this time, I'd scheduled the call for me. I planned to have a discussion about GDS's performance regarding its current and past accounts. IBM Global Services vetted them in the beginning, but I didn't know how relevant their information was today. Before I began, I imparted the sensitivity of my request. We couldn't let GDS know we were snooping for dirt. But I had a solid team and I trusted their discretion.

During the pipeline call, Shelly Finley said, "I might have something." Shelly was one of my strongest client managers. She was tough, smart and could still dominate in field hockey twenty years after high school. We would often joke about how good it felt to dominate opponents almost half our age and how sore we felt the next day. My knees were still aching from the previous week's game in my hoops league.

"Call me at two o'clock," Shelly said. Everyone else committed to investigate and report back, but my money was on Shelly.

Barb buzzed me at 2:00. "It's Shelly."

"What do you have?" I asked.

"Remember that GDS is in Foxhop?" she asked. "They're in year two of a five-year deal. I'm hearing that they won't see year three." A few years earlier, Shelly had Foxhop as a sales rep and had stayed in touch with them.

"That's good, but we only have two weeks at most before the DialTex decision. You still have friends there?"

"I still golf with Kim Brunton."

"I remember Kim, but can you still trust her?" Kim Brunton was a very sharp VP of Tech Services. She reported to the CIO, but Shelly used to say that Foxhop had flip-flopped its organizational chart. Everyone knew that Kim ran IT but internal politics prevented her from getting the CIO position.

"Kim is my Dave," she reassured. Dave was VP of IT Operations at a large bank I covered as a rep years earlier. He loved bourbon and blackjack. I didn't like either, but we shared other vices and he was a big IBM customer. After I left the account, he continued to be an IBM friend that I could count on as a customer reference.

"Wow, I didn't know you guys still partied like that," I joked.

"Stop, you know what I mean."

"No, this is great. See if you can uncover the details of their problems with GDS and ask her if she'll talk. I'll have Hardy call you."

Surprisingly, Dick's meeting with Tony turned into a phone call, but it went okay. They were cordial, and Tony confirmed that our solutions were pretty equal, so it was coming down to price. The word from Dick's office was that he wasn't going to get into a price war with GDS, so we better find a way to win with our solution.

More "help" was on the way. Over the weekend, Dick called an emergency meeting for the entire sales and services team, and we spent much of Saturday and Sunday analyzing our proposal to see where we could bring the cost down. We also looked for competitive advantages to exploit. It was a meaningless exercise done more for cosmetics than results. We had to appear like we were doing everything possible to win this deal; as if we weren't already. Someone from IBM Global Services came up with a "bad press" idea to see where GDS had recently failed. Nothing turned up and I didn't say a word. I wasn't going to let IBM Global Services screw up our plans! It's not that we didn't trust them. They were very good at what they did, but sometimes they tried to involve themselves in things that the account team was best suited to lead.

After IBM acquired a top consulting company, many of their employees had taken leadership positions at IBM Global Services. They were super smart and highly credentialed consultants, but they didn't know IBM very well and some didn't realize the significance of that deficiency. I also questioned some of their sales skills—they were too low on the empathy meter for me. It would take time for the new IBM Global Services to develop a seamless partnership with the sales teams. For now, we had to keep our play with Foxhop very quiet because if it got out that we were not being team players, IBM Global Services could use it against us later if the deal fell through.

The next week Hardy went into action. We were discussing who to hit at DialTex with Shelly's contact. It definitely needed to be a trusted friend, but it also needed to be at least a mid-level manager with enough credibility to recommend IBM as the best solution for technical reasons. The obvious choice was John Rayburn, the manager who had embarrassed us during orals. He was a technically competent manager with the seniority to possibly pull it off—if we were able to convince him. This play alone wouldn't be enough to swing things our way, but if we could sharpen our pencil on price and get Kim Brunton to sell John, maybe the IBM "added value" story would resonate with DialTex.

The next day Hardy called me, furious. "Why didn't you tell me Jerry Dork was coming to meet with DialTex? I just got blindsided by the customer. He's got a 2:00 with Tony and I look like a fool for not knowing."

"Look, slow down! I didn't know!" Things were really getting out of control if I was yelling at Hardy. "Jerry is probably going to cover his butt. He has to look like he's done everything to win this. I'm sure Dick is putting pressure on him, too. I'll call his office to see why we weren't informed. You do damage control."

"Okay, but we look desperate. This isn't good."

"Look, we still have the Foxhop play. How's that going?" I asked.

"That's what I'm talking about. Kim is calling John *today*. This could get out!" Hardy insisted.

"Just take care of John and call me after Dork leaves." I had every confidence that Hardy could handle John. It was just nerve-wracking for him to make a play behind IBM Global Services' back on the same day that our VP of Sales for North America randomly showed up.

"BTS?!" Hardy bellowed the acronym. This was definitely the Burn the Ships moment of our careers.

"You know it!" I replied.

I had to take a deep breath and think, so I took a stress walk around the building. I liked to look at nature when I needed to relax because it reminded me of my childhood in rural Virginia. The birds effortlessly soaring above the trees seemed so at ease. The ducks floating on the lake had it made. *You can't see them paddling ... so never let them see you sweat*, I thought. My mind raced with random thoughts. One day, I would miss these defining moments and the rush I received from doing deals.

Was Jerry Dork dissing us by showing up unannounced, or was it just an oversight? It could be a reflection of what he thought of us or he could just be feeling the pressure of this deal as well. That would be something we would handle later. Right now, we had to go win this deal.

As I walked into my office, I plucked my Mike Forgash trophy and listened to the large silver cup ring. I also stared at The Prospector, a 9-inch statue of a man panning for gold. The Prospector was in my cubical on my first day at IBM and had never missed one of my moves in 10 years. I wasn't superstitious, but these were rituals I used to help me focus.

I called Jerry Dork's administrative assistant and found out that Jerry was in the area and had a cancellation in his schedule. Jerry had called Tony's office to see if he could schedule a quick meeting. They claimed to have called the Managing Director from IBM Global Services to announce the meeting. "IGS must have forgotten to call you," they postured. It all sounded plausible, but I didn't trust anyone now. I checked my daily action list and remembered from the pipeline call that I had to call a customer that was unhappy about a service issue. I was able to squeeze it in before Hardy called at 3:00 pm.

"I've got some good news and some bad news."

"You know I don't like that," I said.

"Sorry, but Dork's call didn't help. He basically told us to get ready for the loss review."

"Loss review? I hope that was the bad news!" A loss review is a post-mortem of sorts where the details of the deal are reviewed to see why the loss occurred, who was to blame and what could have been done to prevent the loss. It is one of the worst activities salespeople have to endure. The tone is cold, subdued and negative. And loss reviews usually take place when there is a previous suspicion that the account team has made mistakes. They're also helpful when an executive needs someone to take responsibility for a loss.

I pounded my desk. "Where in the world is this coming from? We're not going to lose this deal just because Dork had a bad call!"

"I *know* we're not." I could almost hear Hardy's wry smile. "Kim's call went better than expected. She and John hit it off." It turned out that GDS's deal at Foxhop was a case study in why outsourcing deals go bad. There were missed Service Level Agreements, unplanned contract additions, and disagreements about hardware platforms. I always felt that outsourcing was like a marriage—either you grow closer during the contract or further apart. These two had grown apart.

It helped that Kim wasn't a fan of outsourcing. Foxhop's current CIO was using it as a means to cover up his deficiencies, letting someone from the outside run IT so that no one from the inside could steal his power. But Kim was savvy. She was making her play for the crown that was rightfully hers. With GDS out of the way, the current CIO would be exposed.

"But wait, there's more. GDS changed or kicked out two key homegrown apps!" Hardy said, referencing our ongoing infomercial joke. A homegrown application referred to software code written by programmers within the customer's IT staff and not purchased from an outside vendor. I quickly recalled how upset John was when J.R. Winnfield, III dissed his "baby" when Hardy sent the "John is killing J.R." two-way message during orals. John knew his future at DialTex could be in jeopardy if his applications were removed by GDS.

"Dude, you're one lucky son of a gun! This might be a game changer," I said.

"I'd rather be lucky than good," Hardy laughed.

"I'd rather be both. Okay, let's not start celebrating just yet. What's the action?" I said to get us back on track and focussed on the next steps.

"John is so concerned that he's setting up a meeting with his boss and Tony Gaudenza for tomorrow. He wants me to attend."

"Great, but why you? I mean, this sounds like an internal meeting," I said.

"It is. He wants me to hang around outside Tony's office. John knows that if he is successful, Tony is still going to hit us with the price issue."

"Hardy, two things. One, we have to keep this Kim thing quiet. It can't look like we orchestrated all of this behind everyone's back. This meeting with Tony has to look like you were there and suddenly got called in. Two, we can't get in a price war with GDS. Make sure you qualify him."

"So you want to hold my hand?" he quipped.

"I realize that you know what to do, but it's my job to tell you anyway."

To qualify meant to confirm that if Hardy could go back to IBM and get the price Tony requested, we had a deal and Tony agreed he would not shop it with GDS. A top CS like Hardy knew what to do and didn't like being told, but the stakes were now even higher. If our covert operation was exposed during a loss review, leaving IBM would no longer be my choice.

"Let's review the pre-call plan tomorrow morning," I directed.

I left early to have dinner with my family and get in a workout. We could have a decision on this deal by the next day, or, at a minimum, we would at least know where we stood.

The next morning, while dealing with my normal Business Unit Executive duties, Scott, my manager, called. He had heard what Jerry Dork, his boss, had told the team. I asked him to have faith for one more day. This told him that we were working on something that he didn't need to know about.

I called Shelly to thank her for Kim. "Nice work, young lady. This might be the difference in our deal. I'll put $25,000 in it for you if we win." It was coming out of Hardy's commissions, but I knew he wouldn't mind.

"Wow thanks! But you know we discussed something else," she said.

"Are we negotiating? You know that's supposed to happen before the deal is done." I had to tease her a bit before I gave her the good news. "What about a Business Unit Executive job?"

"You found one for me?" Shelly was in line for a promotion and I had been looking for the right opportunity for her.

"Yep. Close by and you wouldn't have to move."

"Stop. Your job? Are you getting promoted?" she asked. "What about Hardy? And are they really going to allow another battlefield in this unit?"

The term "battlefield promotion" was borrowed from the military. During war, if a superior officer was killed in the line of duty, the next senior officer instantly assumed his duties. In corporate America, however, there is usually a promotion process that includes job posting, interviewing, and temporary assignments designed to groom candidates for executive positions. At IBM, it was unusual to see a career path like mine, spanning from entry-level sales rep to Business Unit Executive within the same unit. It was especially unusual for that career path to exclude a staff position or a geographical move along the way. I had been lucky in that regard.

"You're full of questions," I joked. "But first, win or lose, I think my work here is done. Besides, I thought I better get out of here before you and Kim pull a Foxhop on me, too. Second, if we win DialTex, Hardy could grow it into a Managing Director's job. And finally, just because I was promoted from the unit when Donna left doesn't mean we can't do it again. One could argue that it was a good decision. I think things went okay for me."

"You can leave now!" she affirmed.

"Let's talk about this later. We've got a deal to close. I just need to know if you're interested."

Shelly paused for a moment. "Yes."

I hung up with Shelly and immediately began thinking about Hardy's meeting. Anticipating success, I needed to get ready for our price play. I called Will Griffith, the managing director from IBM Global Services, to get the price concession.

Griffith got right to the point. "I'll go a point (1 percent) on price and we can float back another point in a year-end rebate."

"Great, can you send that to me in an e-mail?" I wasn't going to do a back-door play using an IBM Global Services price discount that I received over the phone.

"E-mail? For what? I thought Jerry was going to take this to them on Monday. Why do you suddenly need it now?" He was getting suspicious. I needed to close him hard.

"Cut me a break, Will. I've got Dick calling them mad about price, and Jerry just showing up unannounced. I look bad here." In other words, I was saying, *You owe me one for not telling me about Jerry's call.* "I need to at least appear like I'm in the loop and working with you guys. I need to show something on my pipeline call today." (Remember, it's "their show," the account team is just along for the ride.)

"Mike, I don't know how they slipped on Jerry's call. Okay, I'll send you the note in a minute."

Done. He bought it. Hardy and I were in sync with the flow of our pre-call plan. We were back to the wait stage.

Hardy was called into the meeting about 45 minutes after John and his manager started with Tony.

"Looks like the GDS boys from Texas tripped over their cowboy boots," Tony said to Hardy when he walked in.

"Really? I wasn't aware." Hardy wasn't going to give any hint that he knew about the call between John and Kim Brunton.

"I'm sure you're not. Look, I hope you don't think we're going to do a deal with IBM just because Dick and Jerry showed up a couple of times?"

"Of course not." Hardy was pleased that Tony was true to form and was playing his role in the practiced pre-call plan to a "T". Kiss the Ring, Kneel to Zod, and then go straight into the 5-Ps.

Hardy continued, "I wanted them here to demonstrate how important DialTex is to IBM and to me personally. I've learned a lot and I've enjoyed working with you. Over the last three years, I have been here every day working tirelessly with your team to understand your business and develop solutions to meet your needs. This deal is the culmination of our efforts. I realize we're a bit higher in price, but I'm confident we have the right solution."

There was a long pause. Tony was staring at Hardy and into space simultaneously. The ball was in Tony's court. If Hardy spoke first, he would lose the power. The silence went on for just five seconds, but Hardy said it felt like he clenched his toes for a full minute as he waited.

At last, Tony spoke. "A *bit* higher? You guys have to do better if you want DialTex's business."

"I understand." *Great!* Hardy thought. *There's the price objection. We are getting close.* "So, Tony, if I can go back and somehow convince our management to improve the price by a point, can I tell them that we have a deal?"

"No! Make it two or don't bother coming back," he demanded.

"Wow, two points? Tony, I've got no shot at that. But if I can tell them we definitely have a deal ..."

"Just go get it!" Tony interrupted. Hardy looked at John and John's manager. They nodded.

"Okay," Hardy said and walked out.

He called me as soon as he'd left the room. "I'm playing used car salesman. Tell me you got the concession from Will."

"I got it, Hardy! I'm looking at the e-mail."

"Okay, I'll call you in a minute," he promised.

Hardy returned to Tony's office, but he was gone. John and his manager were still standing there, staring at the phone.

"Tony has his FBC news interview after the closing bell," John said. "Did you get it?"

"Yes. Two points. One as a discount and one in a rebate at the end of the year."

"Done," came Tony's voice from the speaker phone. "Legal has the contracts?"

"Yeah, they've had them for a week," Hardy assured.

"Okay. We'll have them ready with the final changes. Can you get someone here who can sign on your end by one o'clock? I'm going to announce this after closing bell," Tony said.

"Yes, no problem." This was anticlimactic for Hardy. He couldn't believe everything had just come down to an agreement over the phone. And he also realized that we had been played. Tony had been ready to do the deal at the current price. The discount was just to stick it to us.

"Thank you, Tony, I really appreciate your business," Hardy said.

"Okay, just get someone here ASAP." The phone went dead.

"Thanks, guys," Hardy shook hands with John and his manager. "John, I ..."

"You better get going," John interrupted, and Hardy sensed things were getting too emotional for him.

"I'll call you later," Hardy said as he dashed out of the door.

"It's done!" Hardy exclaimed on the phone, almost blowing out my left eardrum. "But those suckers played us. Tony was already planning to announce it after closing bell."

"Son of a gun," I said, laughing. "That just means we both got a good deal. Closing bell? That gives you three hours to get here. Take the train—you drive slower than my grandmother. I'll have Andy pick you up. We've got a show to do! You ready?"

"Yes, I am. I'll catch the 1:30."

The deal was done, but our charade wasn't. We had to ensure that everyone believed we were surprised by DialTex's sudden announcement. The irony of this situation was that we couldn't take credit for closing the deal. I would announce the news to Scott, my manager, and it would go up the ladder. Each management level would prepare their canned response to the question: "How did you close this deal?" [We would all have a different script.] An hour after we closed the deal, Paul White, a colleague, walked into my office.

"How did you guys do it?!" Paul said as he reached out

to shake my hand.

"Man, I don't know. I have no idea how Hardy was so lucky to be in the right place at the right time. He simply got called into Tony's office—the biggest meeting of his career." I erupted in laughter.

"Yeah, right, I bet you don't know."

"Hey, Hardy is on his way here. Tony Gaudenza is announcing it on FBC and I'm having a pizza party for everyone while we watch."

"Cool. I'm in."

During the next half hour my phone rang dozens of times. I told Barb to hold everything. I shut my door and took some time to reflect. "Dude, we struck gold," I whispered to my statue of the Prospector who clutched his pan. My eyes widened as I entered a trance-like state, reflecting on the nine months that had lead up to this moment. *What's next?* I thought.

Barb buzzed. "It's Scott."

I paused, then picked up the receiver. "I told you I needed a day."

"Very nice job on this. You two are unbelievable. Are all of your moves covered?"

"I asked Griffith for a price concession this morning."

"What time?" Scott calmly questioned.

"Around 9:15," I said as I looked at Griffith's e-mail.

"Okay, I'll handle that one, anything else?"

I paused. "No."

Scott also paused, seeming to know there was more but trusting I had it covered. "Congratulations. You guys go celebrate. Take the team somewhere nice. It's on me," he insisted.

At 3:30, Hardy walked into my office. We looked at each other for a moment and then shook hands.

"Nice job," I said.

"I couldn't have done it without you," he replied.

"I think you could have. You're ready for your own unit. But we'll have time to discuss that later. I just talked to Scott and he's prepared."

Hardy's brow wrinkled as he questioned me. "He doesn't know about Kim?"

This was a good time for us to discuss the script. "No, just the price concession, but I could tell he knows there's more. Don't worry, he won't ask you for any other details. You were at DialTex, saw John Rayburn, and he called you into the meeting with Tony. I was already working on the price concession for my pipeline call with Scott when you called me."

Hardy smiled and said, "In other words, we got lucky."

"Exactly. Now that we have rehearsed our lines, let's go put on the show."

Hardy and I went outside my office to an open area where Barb had set up the TV and refreshments. We were just in time.

"And up next is our interview with DialTex's Chief Operating Officer, Anthony Gaudenza," the television reporter announced.

As we entered the room, a crowd of about twenty colleagues paused while scarfing down pizza and soda to applaud and cheer us. Others stood up, peering over their cubicles to witness the scene.

At first, the interview was uneventful. Tony was the usual polished and message-driven company executive who talked around the difficult questions and emphasized the positive parts of DialTex's business. Then, just when I thought he might not announce the deal, Tony interrupted the interviewer.

"I would also like to announce that we have entered into an agreement with IBM to manage our IT. They will assume full responsibility for all of our data centers and call centers. IBM and DialTex will also work together to reengineer parts of our business in order for us to provide even greater products and customer service. Over the last three years, IBM has worked with DialTex to understand our business and develop solutions to meet our needs. This deal is the culmination of our efforts together." The interviewer asked a follow-up question, but the cheering drowned out the audio.

Hardy looked at me and shouted, "He's using my words! 'Last three years' ... 'understand our business' ... 'culmination of efforts'! I said those exact words to him this morning!"

"Well, he must have liked them," I calmly said and gazed back at the TV, applauding.

Hardy suddenly realized he was off-script and turned to high-five a colleague. We would share a moment about this later because it really is validating to have a customer use your words. It's the ultimate compliment a CS can receive. I was very proud of Hardy.

I took the team out for a great evening of dinner and our final deal debrief. This one took place at the bar. Barb arranged a car service so they could celebrate freely. It was great to see the joy on the team members' faces. I could see the nine months of stress being washed off with each round. They deserved it. We all did. We had just closed The Billion-Dollar Deal.

11
THE FUTURE

The deal and celebration were done. Hardy was in line for the Managing Director promotion and Shelly was secretly preparing to take over my job. I got as much satisfaction out of seeing good people promoted as I did closing a big deal. Too frequently I saw the wrong people get the promotion and witnessed the frustration it created. Hardy and Shelly would provide the right leadership and direction in the new IBM culture.

As I sat at my desk and thought about IBM, my rearview mirror was bigger than my windshield. The good old days were gone and not coming back. I became emotionally flat with thoughts about DialTex. There wasn't another Billion-Dollar Deal around the corner. The exposure, lightning quick pace and the adrenalin rush that the deal produced were addictive. I needed something else to motivate me, and my daily duties as a Business Unit Executive could not fill the void. IBM management tried once more to find me something within the company that I would enjoy, but we came up empty again.

In a conversation with Hardy, my decision became clear. He called regarding a personnel issue with one of his sales reps. When that matter was settled he asked, "You still thinking about leaving?"

"I'm thinking about a lot of things, but none of them lead to being a Business Unit Executive much longer."

Hardy saw an opportunity to work on his management skills. "If that's the case, then you only have three options," he said. "One, accept one of the jobs you've been offered here. Two, go work for another company. Or three, go start that company you've been talking about for the last five years. Three is the only option you're going to be happy with, but I don't recommend it in this economy."

"Yeah, I know," I replied. "Everyone has been telling me that. But they caution that finding a new job in this economy is tough, too." No one, including Hardy, knew that I had secretly interviewed and had been offered a job at one of our competitors. The total package was almost 40 percent more than I was making at IBM and they said I could double my salary if I achieved 110 percent of quota, but I turned them down. I had to go through the process, but I was never serious about it. Even if I had been, the process taught me that working for another company would have been a mistake at that time.

"Maybe you should just retire and write a book," Hardy laughed.

After that conversation, I knew what I had to do. Win or lose, I had to try. I planned to leave and start my own company—something I had wanted to do my entire life. I minored in Small Business Management in college and had always planned to leave my first employer after five years to start a company. But the thought of leaving was now daunting—the economy was down, I would need start up funding for the new company, and I hadn't even written a business plan.

The smart thing to do would be to hang around IBM for a while until I was fully prepared, but I wasn't a person who coasted. If I was going to leave, now was the time. I would rather fail than not try. The decision brought an instant rush of adrenaline. *This* would be the definitive Burn The Ships moment of my career. I would not look back. It was time to plot a new course. I struck the match and lit the sails on fire.

Michael D. Maupin

APPENDIX: PRE-CALL PLAN WORKSHEET

190

Watergroup.

This Pre-Call Planning Form is provided courtesy of The Water Group, LLC and can be downloaded at our website.

We hope that it will help you to maximize the productivity of your sales calls and customer meetings.

If you have any questions or would like free expert guidance to help you in your selling process, please visit the new "EXPERT LOUNGE" at our website.

WWW.WATER215.COM

It is recommended that you document AND STORE your PRE-CALL PLANNING answers electronically ON YOUR COMPUTER

BACKGROUND

1 Does this call/meeting feed off of a previous pre-call planning call (is it the logical next call in a sequence of calls to accomplishing your goal(s) for the account)?

☐ Yes, list the date of last call: _____. (If No, go to question #7)

☐ What were the "Next Steps" from the last meeting?

2 Did you accomplish your stated desired outcome for the last call?

☐ Yes. (Skip to question #7)

☐ No. (List the Top 2 reasons why the call failed):

1.

2.

3 Will these 2 reasons prevent you from accomplishing your objective(s) for this upcoming call?

☐ Yes, potentially.

☐ No. (Skip to question #7)

4 How will you address the 2 reasons why the previous call failed?

(Skip to question #7)

THE CALL SETUP

5 What is the prospect/customer's current situation and their near-term objective(s)?

☐ Not sure (Research is needed)
☐ I know the customer's situation (meaning you understand the issues that are important to them today and the challenges that presently affect their business)

Describe:

Customer Business Objective(s): Select:

☐ Improve profitability   ☐ Retain employees
☐ Increase sales   ☐ Improve a process/processes
☐ Reduce expenses/costs   ☐ Improve efficiency
☐ Attract more customers   ☐ Develop, improve skills
☐ Improve customer satisfaction ☐ Alignment
☐ Retain customers   ☐ Learn
☐ Penetrate a new market   ☐ Other

6 What is your ultimate business goal for <u>this customer/account</u>?

☐ Increase sales volume   ☐ Competitive Displacement
☐ Sign them as a customer   ☐ Customer Sat/Retention
☐ Become the primary vendor   ☐ Sign them to a Program
☐ Win the RFP Bid   ☐ Sign them as early adopters
☐ Cross-Sell/Up-Sell   ☐ Get their Involvement in _____
☐ Defend against competition ☐ Other

Describe:

MEETING PREPAREDNESS

7 Can you articulate the value statement of the product, service, or solution you are trying to sell?

- ☐ No (Craft the "So What?" of why your offering is of value to the prospect/person)
- ☐ Yes. Describe:

8 Are you prepared with responses to the top 3 objections you will likely receive?

- ☐ Yes. (List them and provide your answers below)
- ☐ No. (Define them and craft your responses below)

1.

2.

3.

9 Can you articulate high-gain questions related to your call objective that will help you elicit useful selling information from the prospect?

- ☐ Yes. (List them and provide your answers below)
- ☐ No. (Define them and craft your responses below)

1.

2.

3.

10 Can you articulate at least 2 points of differentiation between your MPS offering and your main competitors'?

1.

2.

THE MEETING SALES CALL

11 Based on your ultimate goal for this account (from question #6 above)

A	What will be the focus/discussion topic of this customer call?
B	What is your desired outcome from this call/meeting?
C	How will discussing this topic (described in "A") help you accomplish your desired outcome for this customer call/meeting?
D	How will you know that you have accomplished the desired outcome?
E	How will this outcome ("B" above) move you closer to or help you achieve the goal from question #6 above? If it won't, then consider whether you should have the call.
F	What's in it for the customer? (Why would they care about discussing this topic with you? Why is it worth their time?)
G	Does having this meeting move the customer closer to accomplishing THEIR objectives?
H	What is needed to successfully accomplish your objective(s) for this call?

ABOUT THE AUTHOR

Michael Maupin is an entrepreneur and founder of Marketing and Business Integration (MBI), a sales support and business development firm located in Coatesville, Pa. He is also the Managing Director of MauTiste Investment Group, a real estate development company that specializes in the revitalization of blighted neighborhoods. In addition, he is a Managing Partner in the Water Training Institute, which provides sales training to Fortune 500 companies.

The Billion-Dollar Deal

Look for the next installment in the
Burn the Ships series:

The First Five Million
The entrepreneurial story of Marketing and Business
Integration (MBI).
Coming soon.

The Beginning...